IMPROVISING
BOOGIE-WOOGIE
The Complete Edition

Southern House Publishing

Copyright © 2021 Southern House Publishing

All rights reserved.
No part of this book may be reproduced in any form
by electronic, mechanical or other means
without prior permission from the publisher or author.

ISBN: 978-1-9196118-7-7

tylermusic.co.uk

CONTENTS

Introduction	1 - 2	Rhythmic Triplets	185 - 188
Volume One		Unusual Timing	189 - 195
Key Points	4 - 7	Rolling Chords	196 - 203
Chord Progressions	8 - 9	Walking Bass-Lines	204 - 254
Left-Hand Basics	10 – 11	Left-Hand Patterns 4	255 - 262
Left-Hand Patterns 1	12 - 27	Chord Run Up	263 - 263
Left-Hand Patterns 2	28 - 37	Left-Hand Patterns 5	264 - 273
Left-Hand Patterns 3	38 - 48	Left-Hand Tenths	274 - 274
Left-Hand Patterns 4	49 - 60	Left-Hand Patterns 6	275 - 282
Left-Hand Patterns 5	61 - 67	Adding Some Stride	283 - 294
Left-Hand Patterns 6	68 - 78	Volume Three	
Left-Hand Patterns 7	79 - 87	Left-Hand Patterns 1	297 - 302
Left-Hand Patterns 8	88 - 98	Using Thirds	303 – 320
Minor Chords	99 - 99	Creating Riffs (Thirds)	321 - 323
Walk-Up Patterns	100 - 120	Left-Hand Patterns 2	324 - 329
Left-Hand Patterns 9	121 - 130	Using Sixths	330 - 340
Playing In Other Keys	131 - 135	Scales In Boogie	341 - 362
Transposing Patterns	136 - 142	Twiddly Boogie Riffs	363 - 387
Practice In Other Keys	143 - 147	Creating Riffs	388 - 398
Volume Two		Changing Position	399 - 410
Left-Hand Patterns 1	151 – 155	16/32 Bar Progressions	411 - 422
Adding A Tremolo	156 – 160	24-Bar Progressions	423 - 425
Left-Hand Patterns 2	161 - 166	Practice Suggestions	426 - 427
Left-Hand Patterns 3	167 - 184	Downloadable Audio	428 - 428

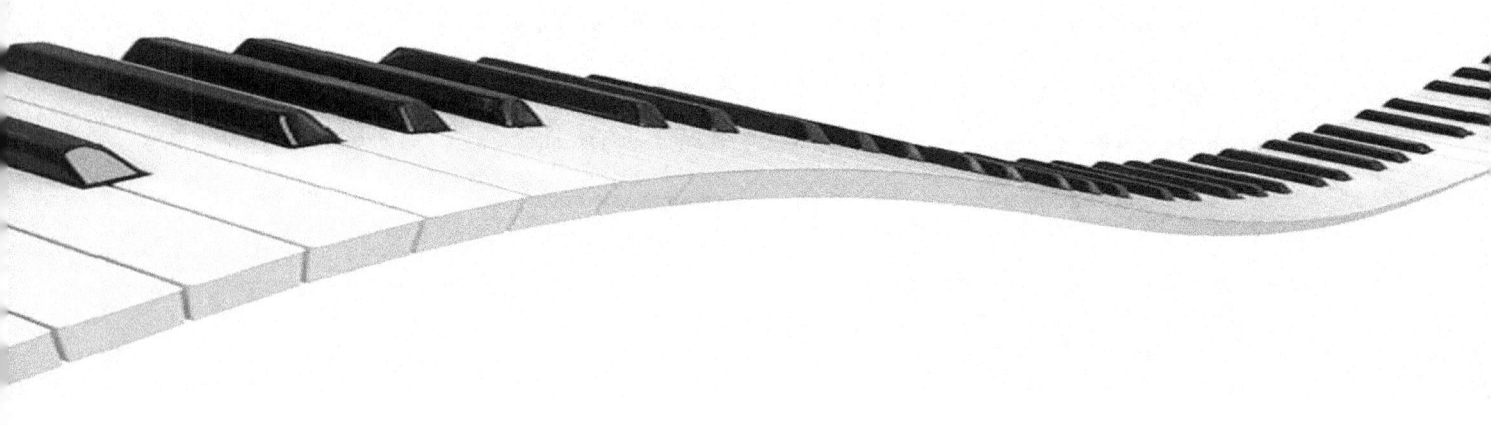

An Introduction

Boogie-woogie is a fantastic and addictive style of piano blues music, that although is no longer mainstream like it was all those years ago, it perseveres within its own niche market. Showing no signs of dying out and still being popular today among those with (dare I say it) good taste in music. So congratulate yourself for being such a person, us fellow boogie people salute you.

Improvising boogie-woogie is for a range of players, designed to suit the beginner to intermediate boogie player and beyond. I don't like to use labels, as they are constricting and often misleading, but we are talking about someone who can obviously read music and play piano, but is still new to the style and interested in learning more. This might be after already having looked at some complete beginner books out there to get started, or someone a little more advanced generally or has already played some boogie-woogie before but wants to know more.

Boogie-woogie is fun to play for sure and there is plenty of sheet music out there available from which you can learn some of the classic songs, but the real beauty of the style is in its improvisational nature, this is where the real fun is.

The series intends to work in two ways, first as an introduction to the music in general and various different styles of playing. Also, to give the reader an insight into improvising boogie-woogie, giving information that they will need to know plus ideas on how to approach doing this, and hopefully the inspiration to do so.

This edition contains all three volumes of Improvising Boogie-Woogie, each one covering different aspects of the style with new information and examples of increasing difficulty as it progresses.

Right then, if you've read all of that I'll simply finish by saying that I hope you find the series helpful but above all else... just enjoy playing, it's what it's all about.

IMPROVISING
BOOGIE-WOOGIE

Volume One

Key Points

Before you step further into the book, there are a couple of points to go over first, just to clarify a few things that will continue on throughout the series.

The Shuffle Feel Notation

Boogie-woogie tends to be played with a shuffle feel, or alternatively you could refer to it as a triplet feel. The music throughout the book is played with a shuffle feel, so it's important to understand how it will be notated before moving any further on.

The music has a kind of long/short jumping sound that gives it the shuffle feel. This is created because each beat has two notes, the first being twice as long as the second. This is created by splitting each beat into three (triplets) but using only two notes, the first note having the value of two triplets and the second one triplet.

Triplet Shuffle Feel

For practical reasons music with a shuffle feel is rarely written using actual triplets like above, instead it's fairly common practice to use straight quavers (8th notes) instead. This is accompanied by a sign (like the one below) telling you that the eighth notes actually denote a triplet feel instead, with the first note longer than the second.

Triplet Feel Sign

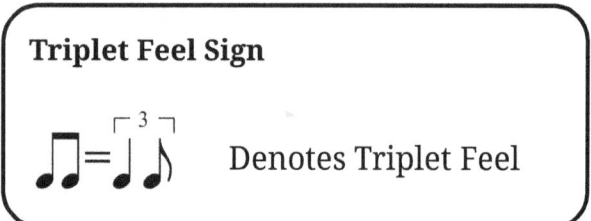 Denotes Triplet Feel

Example Of Notation Using Eighths

You can see below the true value of the eighth notes with how the triplets line up with the straight eighth notes.

This idea might be new to you, or you might have plenty of experience with it already, either way it's simple enough and soon becomes second nature. At times triplets will still be shown it just depends on if they are required or not, but for the majority of the time the book will have the shuffle feel notated as straight eighths.

Putting This Into Context

So let's put this into context with an actual boogie-woogie left-hand pattern. First we have a chopping type pattern notated using triplets (technically correct).

Triplet Notation (Technically Correct)

Next we have the same pattern notated as straight quavers (eighth notes) but with the symbol included denoting the true timing value of the notes.

Eighth-Note Notation

IMPORTANT

Always remember that the eighth notes *are not* eighth notes, they are played as triplets. The first note being long (two triplets value) the second note shorter (one triplet value).

This form of notation has been chosen for the book as it seems to have become the standard way of notating boogie and blues music. It's easier on the eye and once the shuffle feel has been practised for a time it eventually becomes second nature, and you won't even think twice about it.

The Chord Symbols

The chord symbols in the examples are not always indicative of the specific chords within that bar, like '**D13**' or '**D6**' but rather simply show the general chord in order to show the position within the chord progression. This is because, due to the nature of the music the left-hand doesn't always match specifically with the right-hand. You can be moving between all manner of chords within a short space, making it less than practical to be overly specific. Also, with its improvisational nature, it's best to think of the general chord of each bar with regard to the chord progression. Within a bar that is '**F**' for example, you are open to using many versions of that basic chord.

Key Choices

For the most part, the key of choice used here shouldn't surprise anyone. For ease of understanding and explanation the key of '**C**' is an obvious and sensible choice, as it's easier to follow and absorb the information this way rather than use a key with five sharps. The first volume in the series will stay within this one key, although it does have a section that discusses playing in different keys. Of course, ultimately we don't only want to play in '**C**', so to help push things on further, the following two volumes include examples in other keys. Although for obvious reasons we don't have room to cover everything, but some of the more common keys are used to encourage their use.

Fingering Options

Fingering numbers haven't been included here, it wouldn't be practical to do so and besides, anyone here will have some degree of understanding on how to approach the keyboard when given something new to play. There is no all knowing governing body telling us how we should be playing boogie-woogie and the likes of Ammons or Yancy would have just played as came natural to them. If you find a comfortable way to play, and it works well for you then it's probably right, if you are struggling then maybe re-think it. There are certain basic rules to approaching fingering that tend to work well. With the nature of boogie it's best not to limit yourself to a set pattern that may not always be optimal in every circumstance, try to be open and fluid.

Tempo

The speed at which you play the music is (to a degree) up to you. Boogie-woogie might be anything between 100–170 bpm or maybe more (although it can become too fast if you ask me). But, I've stayed away from being too specific regarding speed as this can be off-putting to some and might cause them to try to play something faster than they are ready to. You can match the tempo of the audio examples if you wish, but starting off slower is a good general rule that should be followed. If you listen to boogie-woogie then you will know the kind of tempo that works, but don't rush to play fast. Speed comes as a by-product of accuracy, it comes with time so start at a tempo you can handle and gradually increase it as you improve, don't rush it, just let it happen naturally.

Chord Progressions

Before we start let's have a quick look at some chord progressions used for boogie-woogie. This style of piano is closely related to the blues – being an off-shoot variant – so it quite naturally uses similar chord progressions, in-fact a lot of boogie-woogie in general is transferable to some degree. You might already be well aware of these but here's a quick reminder of the most commonly used ones. It's a good idea to have them memorised, but don't threat about it as that will happen in time with continued playing.

1.

The most simple of the twelve-bar blues progressions.

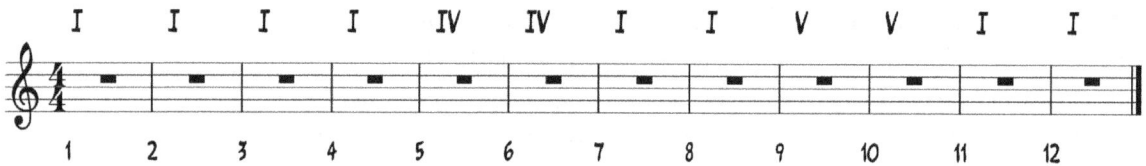

2.

Here bar-ten swaps to the '**IV**' chord.

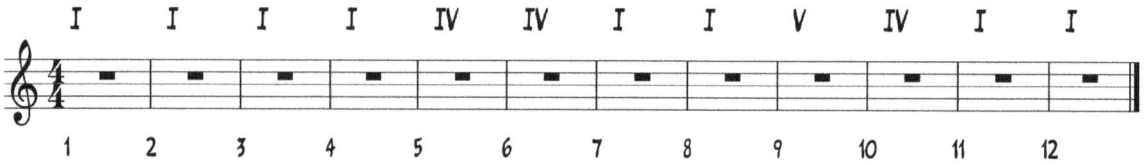

3.

Here bar-two is changed to the '**IV**' chord.

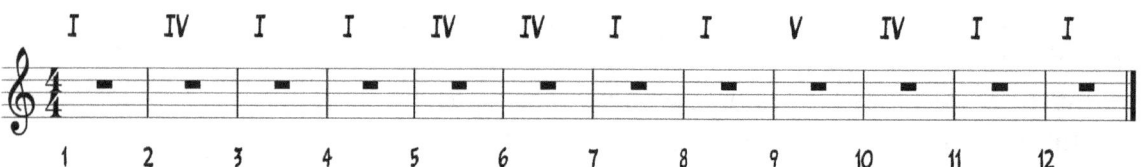

4.

Here the last two bars each have chord changes.

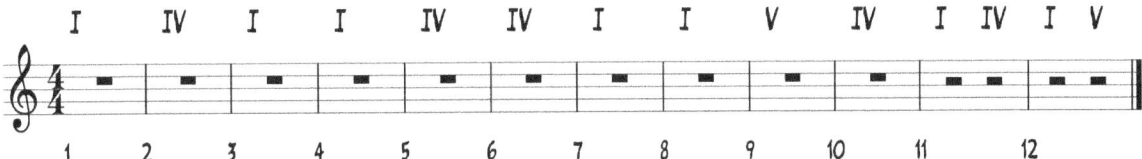

5.

Here bars nine and ten are changed to the 'II' chord and 'V' chords respectively. This doesn't work with everything, but it does work nicely with a walking bass-line.

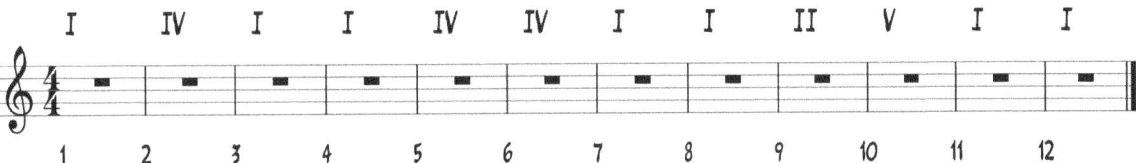

6.

This progression is the same apart from the last bar which has been changed to the 'V' chord.

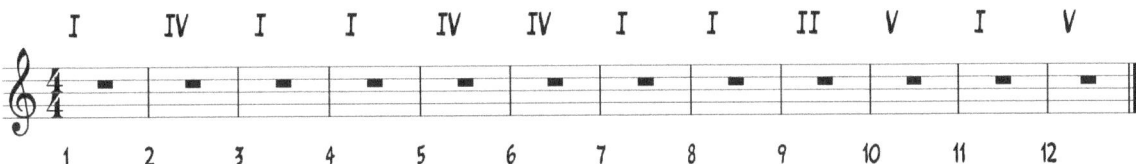

NOTE

The first three of these are by far the most commonly heard progressions and so you might want to concentrate on them to begin with before changing/adding other things. It is of course quite possible to mix things up even further, but that isn't something to start with and if you go too far you can step away from what might be considered proper traditional boogie-woogie piano. Although there isn't anything wrong with that, it's just down to taste.

Left-Hand Notes

The majority of boogie-woogie bass-lines consist of a repetitive pattern that tends to span one bar, there are of course exceptions. Naturally they contain the root note of the chord but beyond the root note there are a number of notes that are commonly used. Whilst you don't need to know anything about the nuts and bolts of music to simply copy and play, it will help a tremendous amount in taking a step further into improvising and when transposing things into different keys. So while it may not seem as interesting as just knocking out some good old boogie, it's important to know the nuts and bolts of the music in the long run. The best way to do this (rather than get bogged down) is to learn little bits at a time as you go along, it's all quite basic stuff really.

The usual suspects when dissecting a boogie bass-line are shown below, and they stem from a mix of different scales. The example here is in the key of 'C' for simplicity.

Most Commonly Used Notes

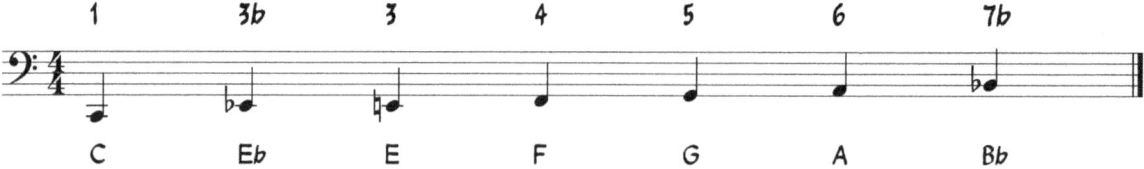

You can see a large portion of these are from the major scale, with the root, third, fourth, fifth and sixth all used. You may also notice that the majority of the major scale is included, and only two notes tend to be omitted, being the second/ninth and the major seventh.

Common Notes From The Major Scale

The other two notes that are most commonly used can be found within the minor blues scale, these two are the minor-third and the flat-seventh.

Additional Notes From The Minor Blues Scale

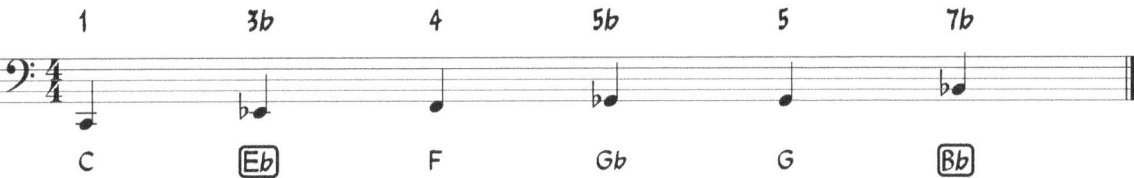

You might notice that the minor-blues scale also includes the root, fourth, and fifth from the major scale.

Notes Commonly Used From Major Blues Scale

Most of the common bass notes are also found within the major blues scale, as shown below.

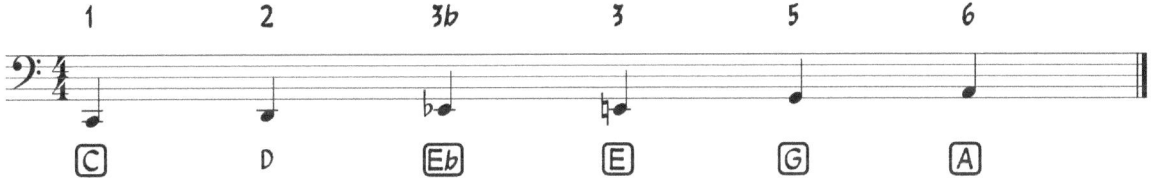

Be careful not to forget or neglect the major blues scale, it's an important part of boogie-woogie music and contains many of the commonly used notes. Unlike the minor-blues scale it includes the 'second' being the '**D**' in the key of '**C**'. This isn't so commonly used with the left-hand, but it can be used on more complex patterns or walking style patterns.

NOTE

Remember, this isn't vital to know to simply play the music but if you aim to improvise, transpose into other keys, transcribe the music from recordings or create your own songs, then it becomes important.

Left-Hand Pattern 1

We will begin here with this good old left-hand which is certainly one of the first that everyone learns, so you might well be quite comfortable playing this already.

It begins with the root and fifth, moves to the root and sixth before returning to the root and fifth again. As you can see, it moves from a nice safe consonant sound (both being chord tones) to the more dissonant sound of the sixth. All notes are from the major scale and shown in key of '**C**'.

Have a practice of this over a twelve-bar blues progression. If this is new to you, remember that it's played with a shuffle feel and not straight-eighths. The most important thing about this is keeping the timing and feel even and consistent throughout. This may seem simple but really concentrate on the feel of that left-hand. Listen to it, really think about it and ask yourself... Does it have that proper bouncing shuffle sound? Is the tempo consistent? Does it sound like the music recordings you listen to?

Use a metronome to begin with, start off slow and gradually build up the tempo, but make sure you keep the triplet shuffle feel as you play faster.

12-Bar Practice Example

IMPORTANT NOTE

Although this left-hand pattern is technically quite simple and so appears easy, it isn't quite as easy to play well. To do this well consistently, actually takes an awful lot of practice. You want to be able to play it in your sleep without thought, keeping the timing and feel consistent throughout, slow or fast while playing/improvising anything that comes to mind over the top. It's not technically hard, but takes practice.

The next example adds the right hand to the left, using a common chord movement. The right-hand is matching the shuffle feel of the left-hand with the idea of helping to reinforce the feel/rhythm of the music.

Remember, it doesn't matter how complex or impressive the right-hand is if the left-hand falters. If the general feel isn't right then the whole thing falls apart, it's the backbone of the music. Don't expect to sound great straight away necessarily as everything takes time and practice.

12-bar Practice Example

Optional Ideas

Shorter Duration

A couple of things to play around with and consider. Here the long and short notes are played for the same duration with a triplet rest in-between.

Basically aim to keep the notes crisp, more staccato in nature. This is one way to play that you can hear on recordings, but the difference is only really noticeable at a slower tempo. In reality this is actually how the left-hand is at a high tempo, as you don't have the time to physically hold the keys down any longer than this in order to hit the following keys.

Accented Notes

At a slower tempo it is possible to accent the notes if you desire. Below shows the second and fourth beats being accented, it's only a minor difference in volume, but it arguably drives the bass along a little.

> **NOTE**
>
> None of this is relevant at the normal frenetic pace of the average boogie piece, but something to play around with if you feel like slowing things down somewhat. At a higher tempo of perhaps 140 – 160 bpm, those first notes will be played short and crisp anyway due to the limited amount of time you have available to physically play them before moving to the following keys.

Comping Patterns

As well as looking at the melodic side of boogie-woogie we are also going to concentrate some time on the rhythmic side in the form of comping patterns.

Now there are probably different definitions of this word flying around and different terms for what I am talking about, so to clarify when I say comping I'm referring to simple rhythmic patterns that are usually played with chords. The kind of thing you play to fill in or accompany someone else, nothing overly complex or fussy. Some people might use the terms 'pad' or 'vamp' but in the end we are talking about a series of rhythmic patterns that are repeated over a series of chords that fill in rather than being overtly melodic.

It's a good idea to practice these and get them ingrained upon your subconscious mind as it enables you to drop them into your playing at any time. This sort of thing can be heard in boogie-woogie either as complete sections (often a whole twelve-bar sequence) or used in-between melodic parts.

Comping Pattern. 1

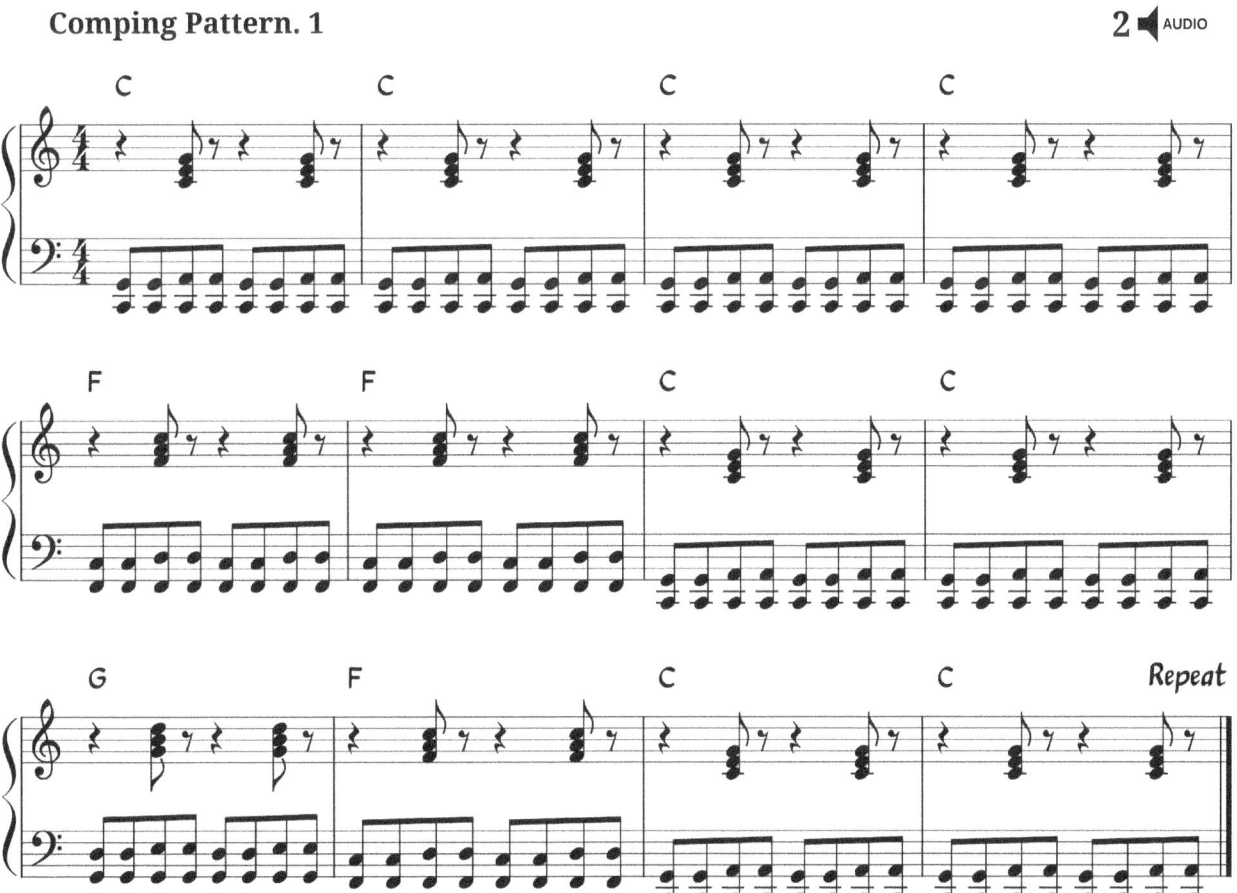

Common Chords

Using straight major chords is fine, it works, but we need to make things more interesting by adding a little something and the use of sixths, sevenths, and ninths works wonders. Don't forget to use the different inversions when you play instead of getting too attached to one in particular.

Sixth Chords

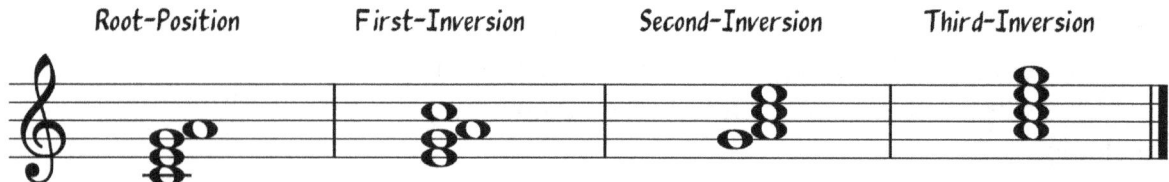

Seventh Chords

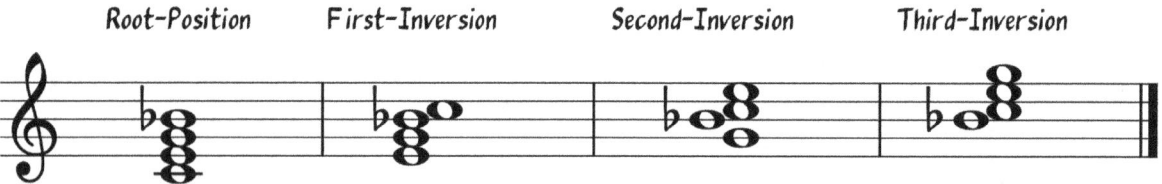

Ninth Chords

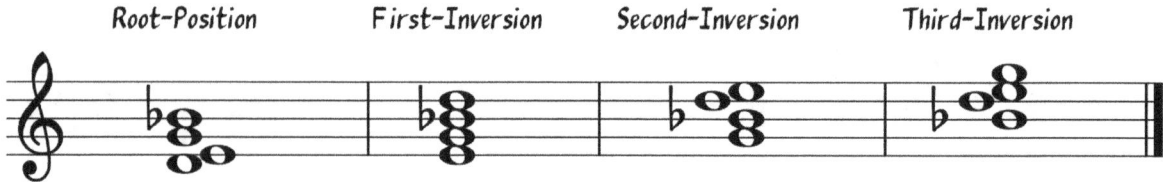

Comping Pattern. 2

Comping Pattern. 3

Comping Pattern. 4

5 AUDIO

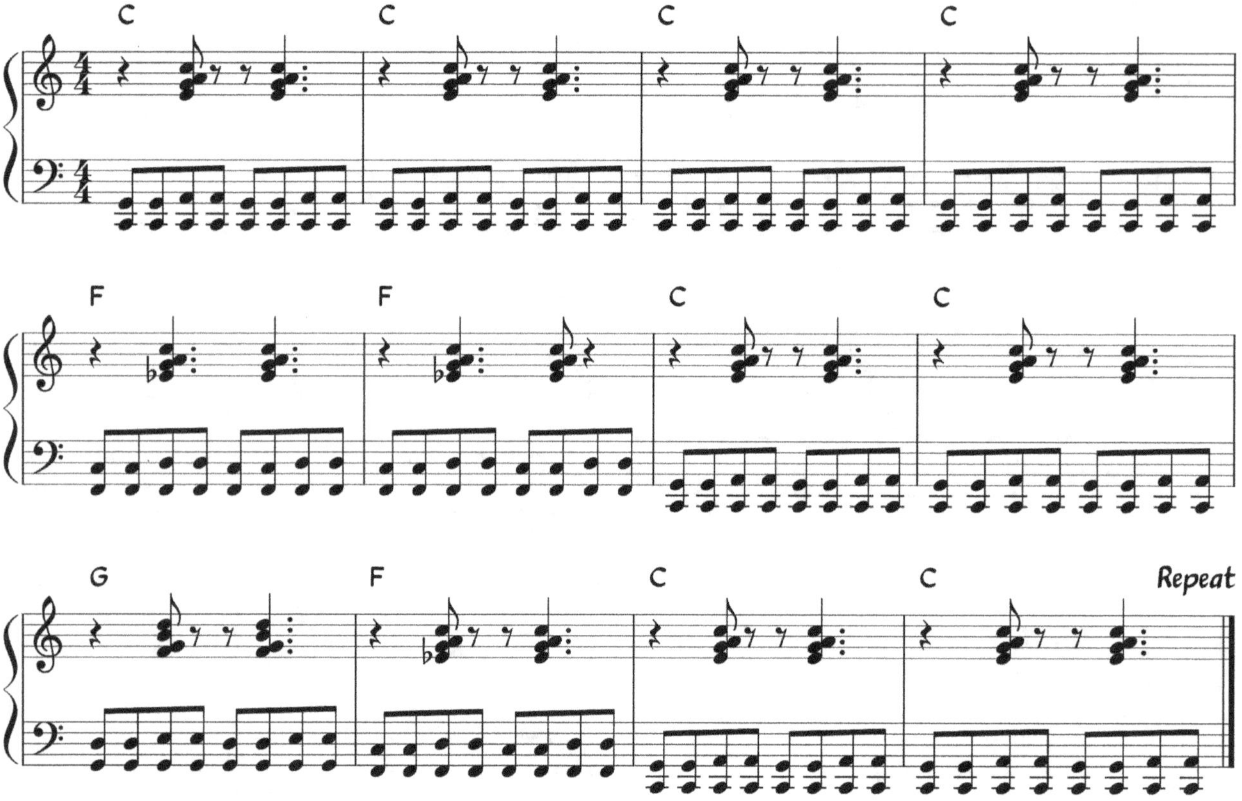

Comping Pattern. 5

6 AUDIO

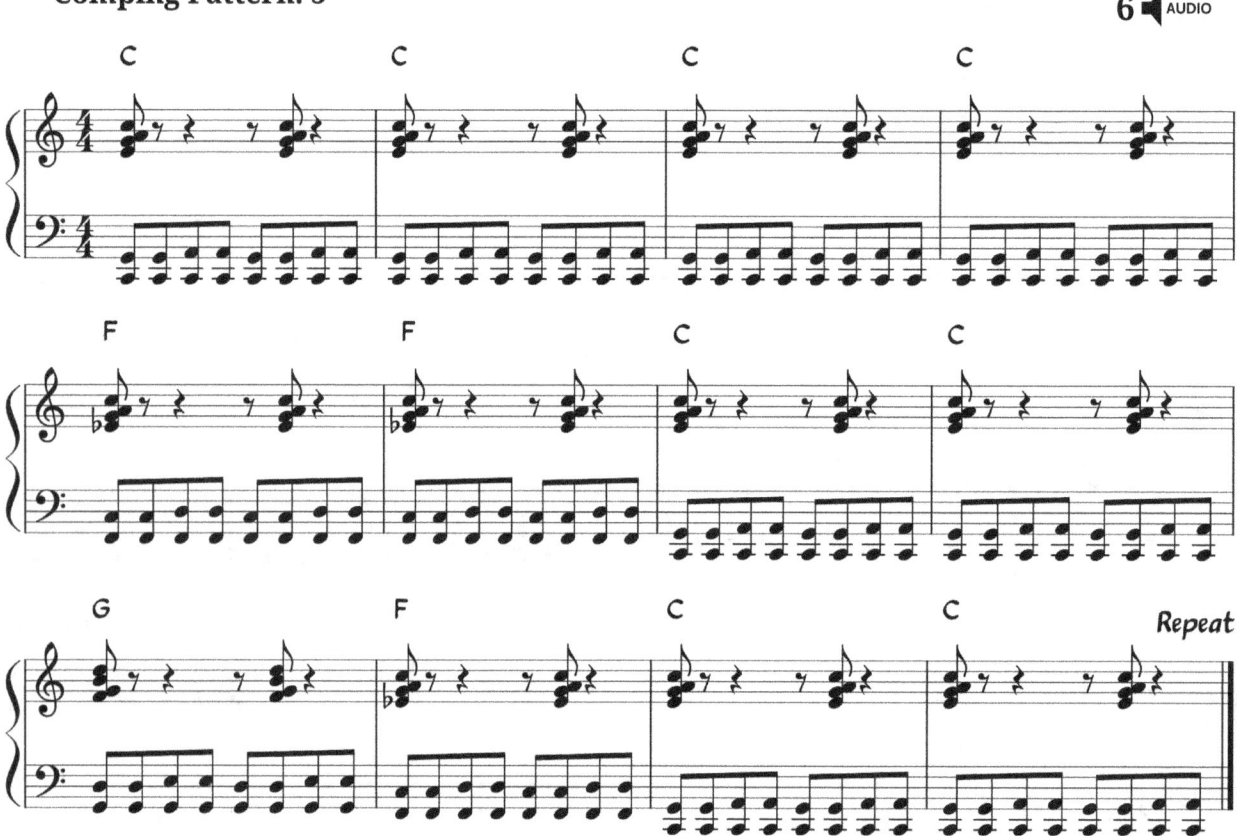

Chord Movement (Sixth To Ninth)

The ninth chord sounds great in boogie-woogie, and while you can play these in several inversions, there's an easy chord change to remember. When coming up to the 'IV' chords, you only need to drop the third of the preceding 'I' chord a semi-tone down to create it.

Shown In Key Of 'C'

>>>Third moved down one semi-tone>>>

The dropped third (on the 'I' chord) becomes the seventh of the new 'IV' chord, the fifth becomes the ninth, the sixth the third and the root the fifth.

Shown In Key Of 'G'

>>>Third moved down one semi-tone>>>

Shown In Key Of 'A'

>>>Third moved down one semi-tone>>>

This simple movement is quite easy to remember and makes the chord change really simple to play, and so quite easy and useful to throw in while improvising.

Comping Pattern. 6

Chop That Boogie

Make Time To Boogie

Left-Hand Pattern 2

So now we have had a look at the most common left-hand pattern, it's time to add a little something to it.

Let's look at the same pattern again. It's absolutely fine as it is and pretty much ubiquitous in boogie and blues (being heard on recordings since the dawn of time) but once you've mastered it a little, you will want to play around further.

As discussed before, it uses the root, fifth and sixth, so what can we add to change it?

Looking at the minor blues scale we have the seventh at our disposal, so we can add that to the bass pattern to create something new.

Flat-Seventh From Minor Blues Scale

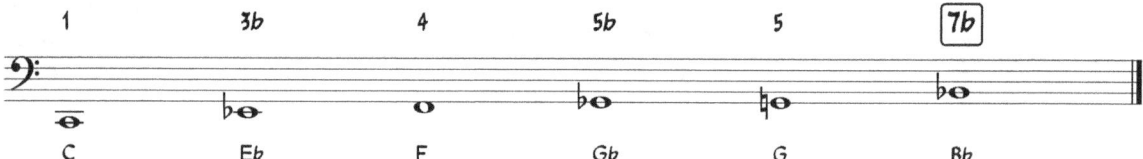

Below you can see how you have the same basic pattern but the flat-seventh has been added on the third beat. There are quite a number of different combinations you can use here.

> The following examples retain the basic feel of the original chopping style left-hand, they don't alter it completely, they just add a little to it. As always it's recommended to practice with a metronome to keep the timing on point, start off at a tempo you can manage easily and gradually speed up.

Bass Pattern 2.1

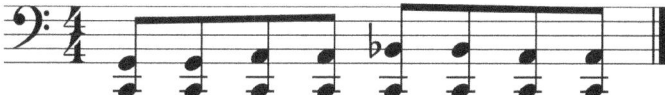

The flat-seventh is used on beat three replacing the fifth.

Bass Pattern 2.2

The flat-seventh is used on beat two for a single note.

Bass Pattern 2.3

The flat-seventh is now used on beats two and four, doubling up on the previous pattern.

13 AUDIO

Bass Pattern 2.4

Here the flat-seventh is only used on beat four.

14 AUDIO

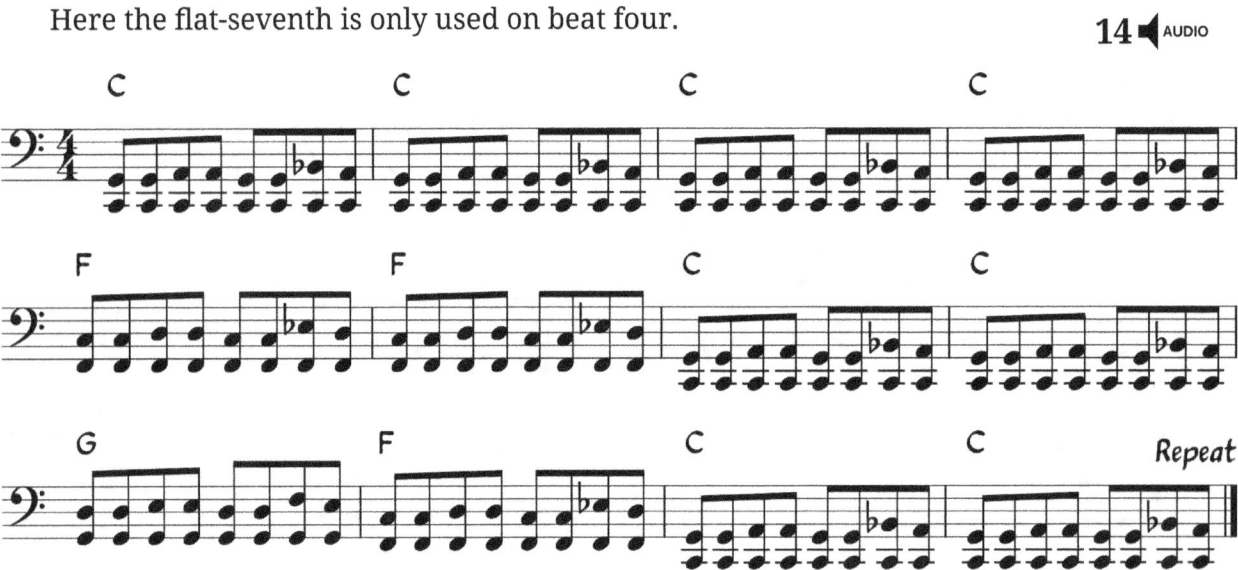

Comping Pattern. 8

15 AUDIO

Comping Pattern. 9

16 AUDIO

Comping Pattern. 10

Comping Pattern. 11

Combinations

You could use any of those patterns individually, or you could alternatively combine them. I wouldn't add all of them together at once, as that would overly complicate things, and a good boogie-woogie bass-line needs to have a degree of consistency. But to make things a little more interesting, you can certainly change up the odd bar here and there. One way is to add a little something at chord changes.

Example. 1

Example. 2

Chopping Board Boogie

Left-Hand Pattern 3

Using the flat-seventh with the left-hand isn't the only option of course and looking at the minor blues scale below we can see the flat-third could offer some interesting possibilities.

Flat-Third From Minor Blues Scale

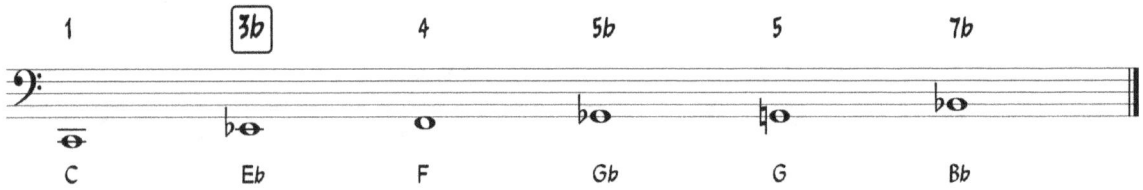

Bass Pattern 3.0

This pattern retains the first three beats of the original but adds the flat-third on beat four, although it quickly switches back to the third. It's that constant switching between consonant and dissonant sounds that makes music interesting.

Bass Pattern 3.1

Here you have essentially the same thing but the section with the flat-third has switched position, now being on beat-two instead of beat-four. The constant switching from the minor-third to the third is a common thing in boogie-woogie and is also used a lot with the right-hand too.

Bass Pattern 3.2 22 🔊 AUDIO

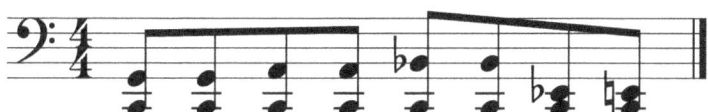

This pattern uses a combination of both the flat-third and the flat-seventh, being used on beats three and four.

Bass Pattern 3.3 23 🔊 AUDIO

Now this left-hand pattern stands up quite well on its own without being used in conjunction with the others, so it could be the basis of an entire boogie piece rather than an add-on.

Bass Pattern 3.4

This is essentially the same pattern, but it has removed the root note on beats two and four. It makes a somewhat lighter sound and most boogie left-hands sound best with the root pounding away below to some degree, but it's certainly an option. It works well at really high tempos where playing the root note continuously becomes more difficult physically.

Comping Pattern. 12

Further Combinations

Combination. 1

Combination. 2

Combination. 3

Combination. 4

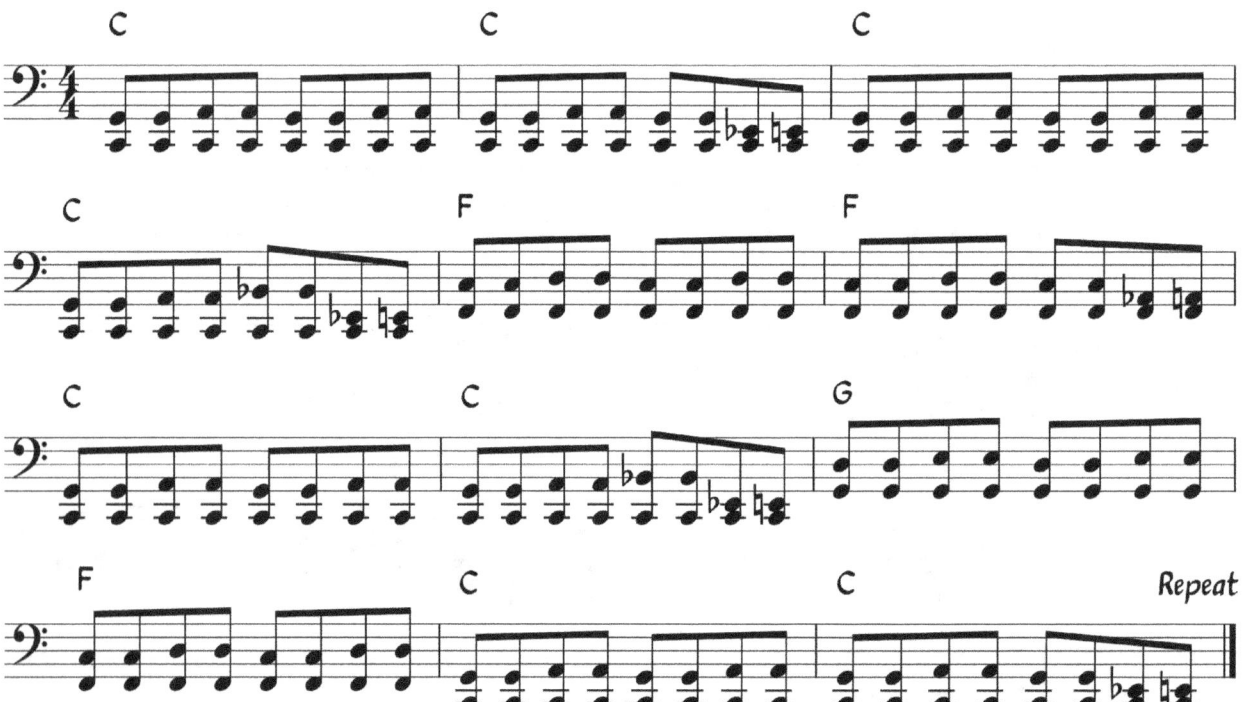

Combination. 5

Combination. 6

Hot Chop Boogie

Left-Hand Pattern 4

This pattern is a variation on the previous one, although it has been separated here as it is arguably quite a common/popular one that stands out on its own and is also the basis for a number of others.

Variation

You can also play this without the root note on the second and fourth beats. The resulting sound is without a doubt weaker than with them, but it does allow you to play the pattern at a much faster tempo easier.

Have a practice of this without the right-hand until it falls comfortably under your fingers. Below is the full version with the root note included on every measure, but you can play the alternative version if you prefer. Ideally, perhaps practice both of them instead.

Practice 12-Bar Progression

Comping Pattern. 16

Comping Pattern. 17

Variations

This variation changes the last beat to include the root/sixth and the fifth instead of repeating the same flat-third and third combination. You can use this pattern on its own if you wish (it works well) or you can incorporate it in with the original version. I would suggest practising it both ways.

Combination. 1

Combination. 2

Six Way Boogie

Linking The Changes

You may notice from playing the pattern we have been looking at that it can be awkward sometimes at the chord changes (dropping from the '**F**' to the '**C**' chord for example). Getting the thumb back down in good time to play the fifth of the '**C**' on the first beat of the new chord isn't necessarily the easiest of things when playing at speed.

A common way around this is to pre-emptively change to the new chord on the bar that precedes the new chord.

1.

See how this chord change has the last note of the '**F**' chord replaced by a note from the '**C**' chord in the following bar.

2.

The same idea here for the '**V**' to '**IV**' chord change.

3.

It's also possible to use the same idea within the pattern without a chord change being present.

> **NOTE**
>
> The tie on the note that bridges the two bars is optional, you can just repeat the note if you wish, but I like the way the tie sounds plus it smooths the transition over the keyboard.

Bar Tied Example. 1

Have a practice with this idea over a twelve bar progression, it sounds good and also makes playing over the keyboard a little smoother.

Bar Tied Example. 2

You don't have to necessarily do this on every chord change, so here the tied pre-change note is only found on the chord changes that are moving down the keyboard.

Chord Tie Example. 3

Another – perhaps obvious – option is to use a tie on each bar and carry that joining note over every time. Personally I like it this way as it flows nicer.

Chord Tie Example. 4

One last variation on this theme sees the bass pattern move upwards to include the seventh again. This is used here at the chord changes 'I' to 'IV' and 'I' to 'V' and also at the end of the twelve bars leading into the repeat.

Comping Pattern. 18

33 AUDIO

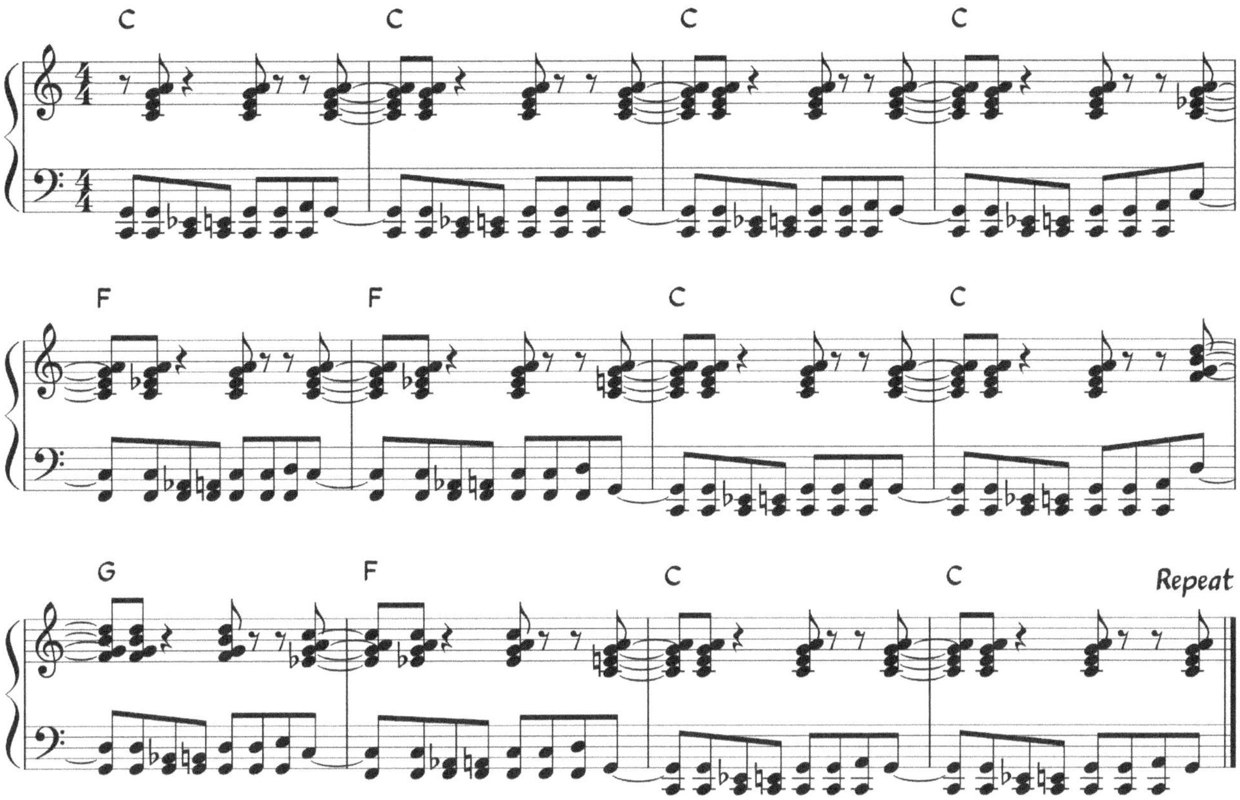

Comping Pattern. 19

34 AUDIO

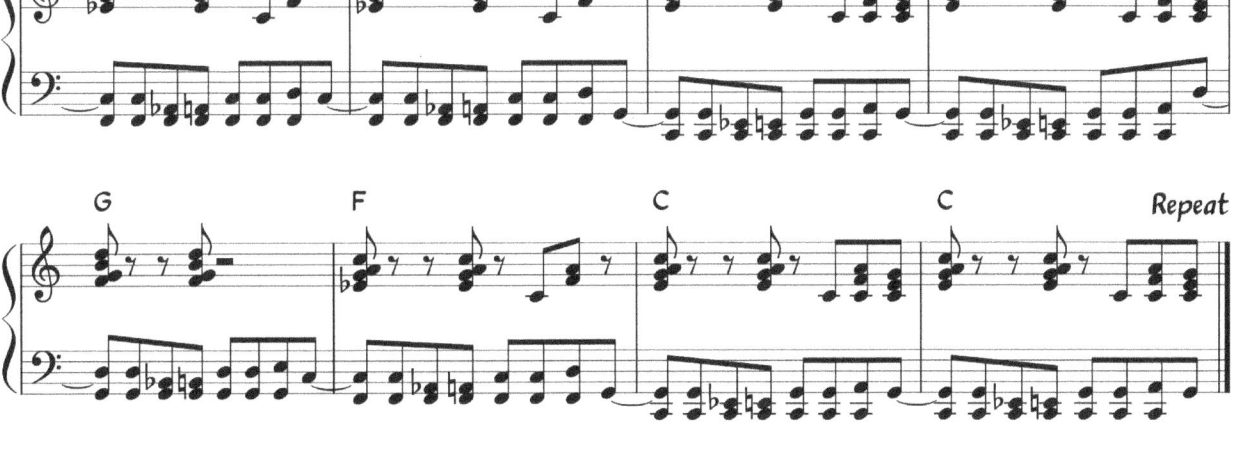

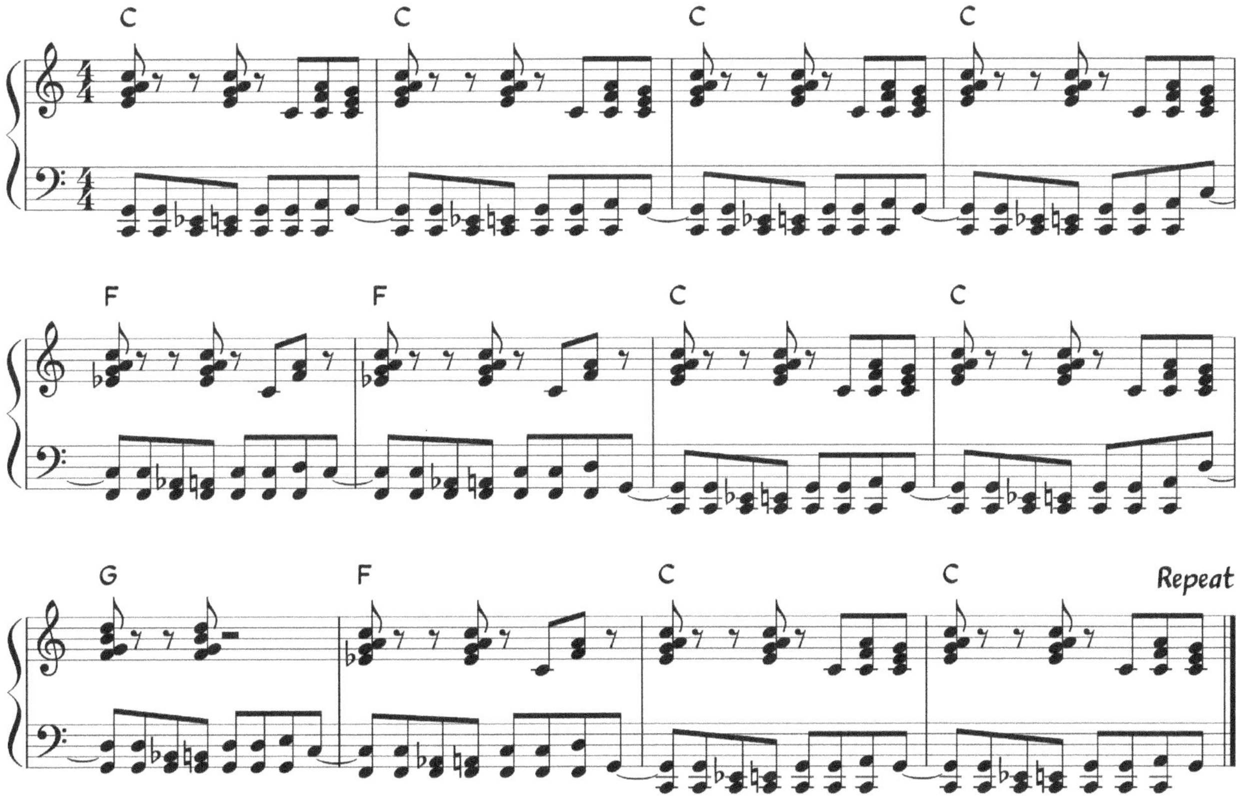

Comping Pattern. 20

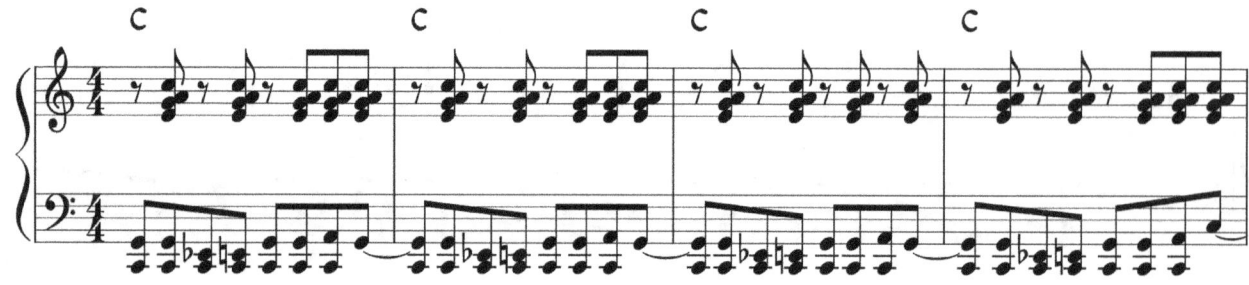
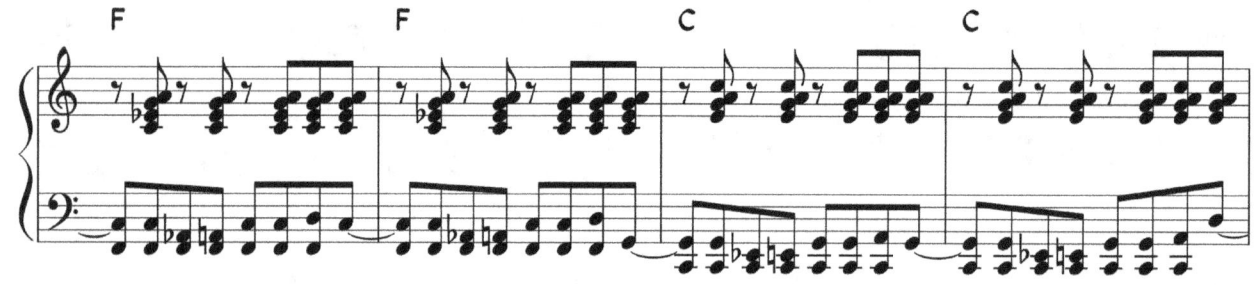

Left-Hand Pattern 5

Moving on to a new pattern, this one is slightly unusual in that it starts on the fifth rather than the root note of the chord.

Because of this, when you begin playing it's common place to include the root note on the preceding bar to lead into it. Once within a piece the preceding bar ends with the root note anyway, so it just continues on and on.

12-Bar Chord Progression

36 AUDIO

> **NOTE**
>
> This can be played fast like most boogie-woogie, but I'm also a fan of this particular one when it is slowed down somewhat. I think this is how I remember first hearing it played, but by all means play it faster if you wish.

Sleepy Boogie

This is intended to be played at a slower tempo than the average boogie-woogie (perhaps 100 bpm to 120 bpm). As is quite common there is movement between minor-thirds and major-thirds with the 'V' chord incorporating diminished and major chords.

The left-hand movement at the chord changes can feel quite awkward when played as in 'Sleepy Boogie', so here's a better (although optional) way of playing. Pre-empt the chord change and play the root note of the next chord as the last note prior to the chord change. This is an idea that we looked at previously and makes the transition between chords easier and smoother.

Another Variation

A further alteration shown below adds a little something extra to the pattern. This could be used in conjunction with the original version or on its own.

This changes things somewhat, as now the bar begins with the root note instead of the fifth, which is also now played twice. This works best if it's only used every other two-bars rather than repeating that double root note every-time. Practice it over a twelve-bar progression shown on the next page.

Twelve-Bar Practice

To further change the feel of this pattern another way to play is to tie over the preceding note from the previous bar, so the fifth is held while you begin the double root notes.

Held Over One Note

Held Over Both Notes

> **NOTE**
>
> It doesn't make much difference which version you use, the difference is so small it's barely noticeable, but I thought I'd show both and let you decide how you would like to play it. Practice them over a twelve-bar chord progression as shown on the following page.

Tied Over Variation. 1

Pattern with the fifth tied over into the following bar.

Tied Over Variation. 2

Another little variation could have you moving up to the seventh at the end of the pattern. Shown here at the end of the 'I' chord as you move to the chord change. Don't do this too often, but it does create more interest.

Laid Back Boogie

Left-Hand Pattern 6

This particular pattern was found on some early recordings by Pete Johnson for one. It uses the root and fifth along with the sixth and third.

12-Bar Practice Example

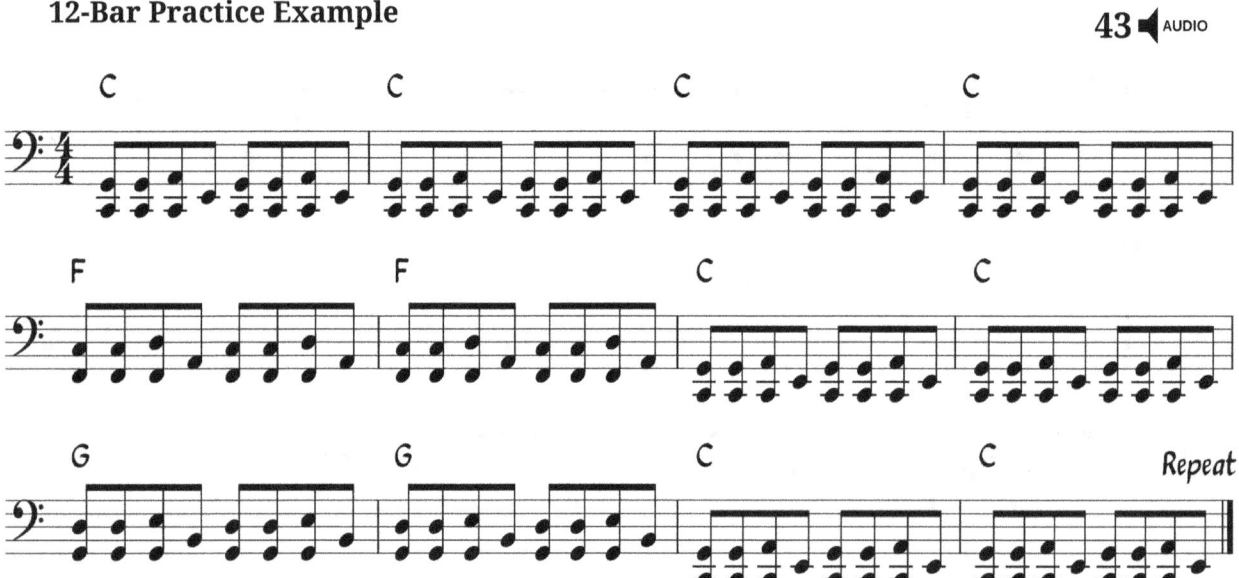

> **Optional Variation**
>
> You could play this with the root note added to the third if you prefer (probably sounds a little better). I'm not sure if Mr Johnson did this or not from the old recordings, but it works well either way.
>
>

Variation. 1

In addition to this you could make an alteration at the chord changes. You wouldn't use this on every change rather just add it occasionally for variation when you feel like it, or indeed don't add it at all.

12-Bar Chord Progression

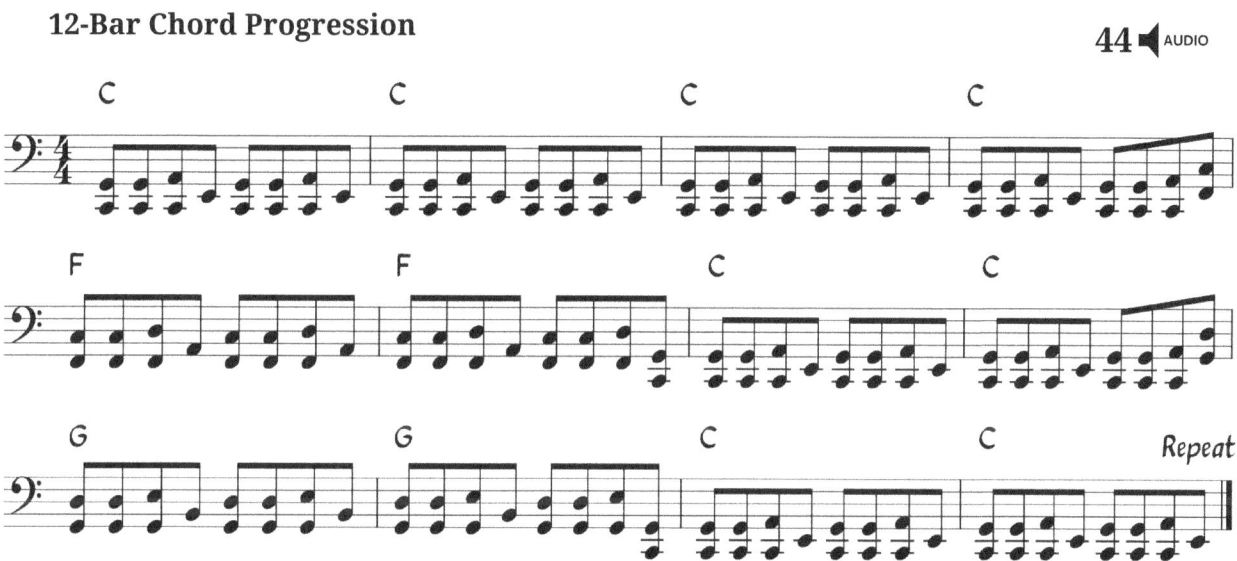

Alternative 12-Bar Chord Progression

Comping Pattern. 20

46 AUDIO

Comping Pattern. 21

47 AUDIO

Double The Boogie

Midnight Boogie

Left-Hand Pattern 7

Moving on to a new pattern we return to the common root and fifth being played together, but now we are combining the flat-third and the sixth together. These sound pretty good with their dissonant sound resolving to the third.

12-Bar Chord Progression

Alternatively you can add the root note to the third, you may or may not prefer this. Although it's not a massive difference some people like the left-hand as large and full as possible.

Variation With Additional Root Note

Try both versions out and see which one suits your own playing, there isn't a right or wrong here, although I'd suggest practising both. The lighter version is perhaps easier on the hand at higher tempos.

Additional Root Note 12-Bar

51 AUDIO

Variation. 1

This has the flat-seventh combined with the flat-third. It's quite a fussy pattern but interesting to play around with. It could be used singularly or alternatively combined with the previous versions.

12-bar Practice Example

52 AUDIO

Variation. 2

12-bar Practice Example

53 AUDIO

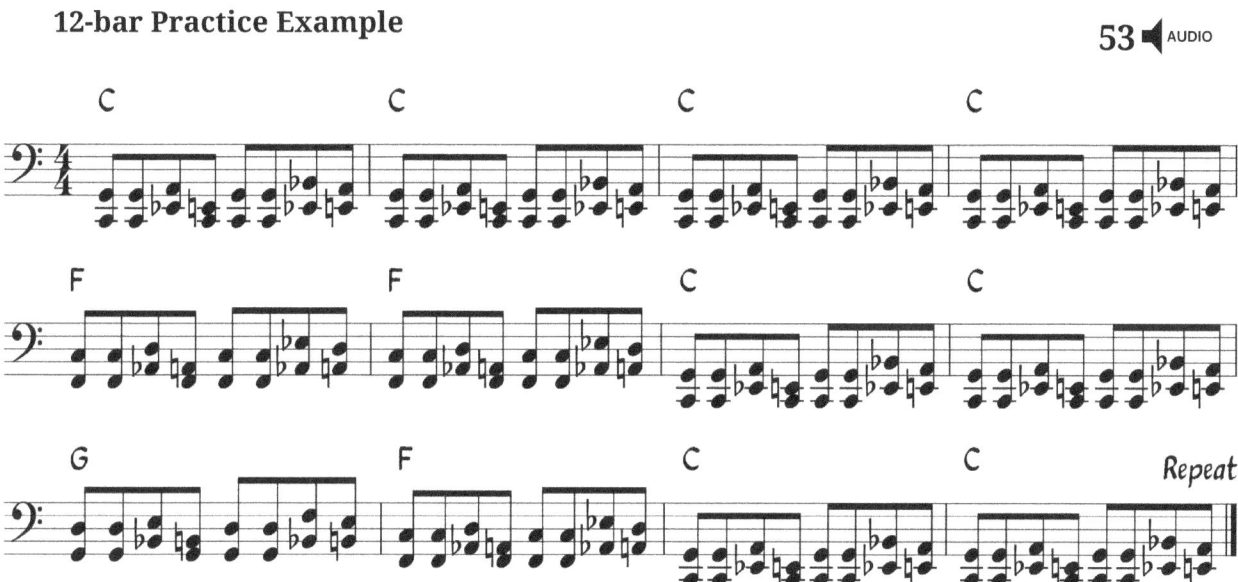

Variation. 3

12-bar Practice Example

54 AUDIO

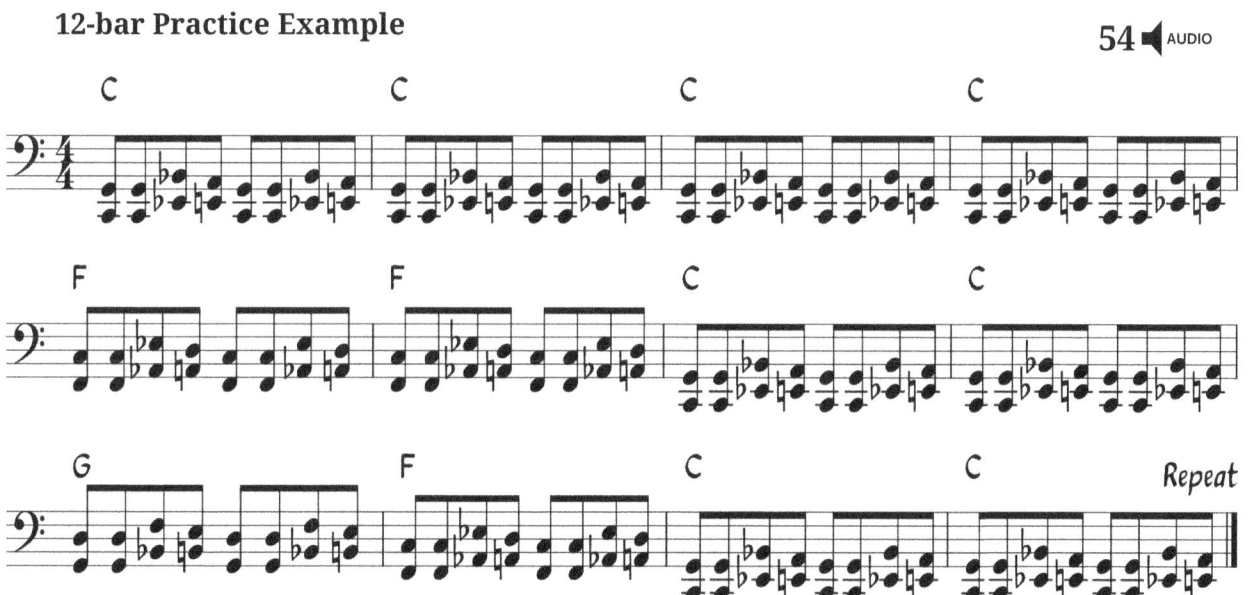

Combination/Switch

If you find the last example a little too heavy to use through an entire piece, it can still be put to good use. One thing you can do is swap the left-hand pattern to something different at times. This can be a complete change (like swapping to a walking bass or some stride) or it can just be a version of the main pattern, it's just a little something to mix it up with.

Pattern. 1

This is what we are going to begin with and revert back to.

Pattern. 2

The pattern we are going to switch to mid-way.

Pre Switch Lead In

Often you might hear something added that leads into a change. Sometimes it can be something dramatic and othertimes something quite subtle like the examples below, which use a selection of the same notes.

1.

2.

Switching Patterns Practice Example

Monday Blues Boogie

Left-Hand Pattern 8

This is a well known pattern that anyone whose listened to much boogie-woogie will have no doubt heard. It's been used by pretty much everybody since its inception many years ago, and for good reason, it's great.

It's created using the root, third, flat-third, fourth, fifth and sixth, yes it's pretty busy this one.

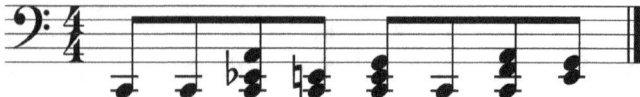

It's worth pointing out that you hear people play this in slightly different ways. The example above is arguably the more complete (perhaps original) version, but it can be played differently, often with fewer notes as shown below.

Alternate Version. 1

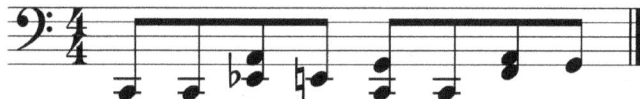

Alternate Version. 2

Alternate Version. 3

Take your pick, although there is plenty of disagreement regarding how this was originally played. I'd concentrate on practising the pattern in its fullness (although between you and me the odd dropped note won't be noticed by most people). Ultimately there is no real right or wrong, if it sounds good, and you're happy with it, play it.

12-bar Practice Example. 1

You might prefer to begin with a lighter version of this pattern until you become comfortable with it. That's up to you of course, but it's often best to start small and move from there once you're ready.

12-bar Practice Example. 2

Here you have the fuller version to practice over a standard twelve-bar progression. You can see just looking at it how much busier it is, although the rhythm and hand movement is much the same, so it's not too much different to actually play.

Comping Pattern. 22

58 AUDIO

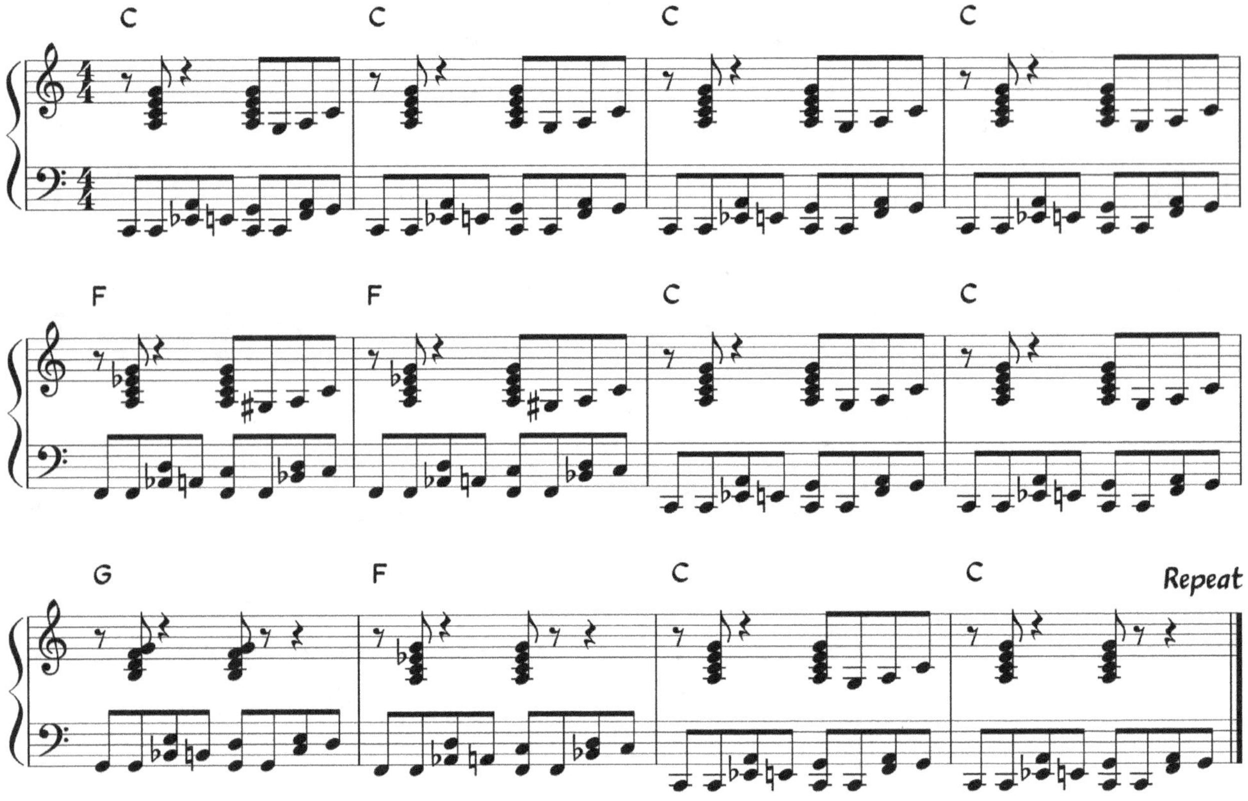

Comping Pattern. 23

59 AUDIO

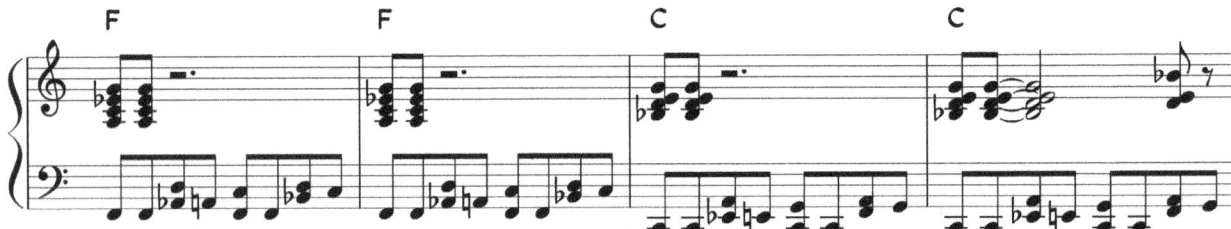

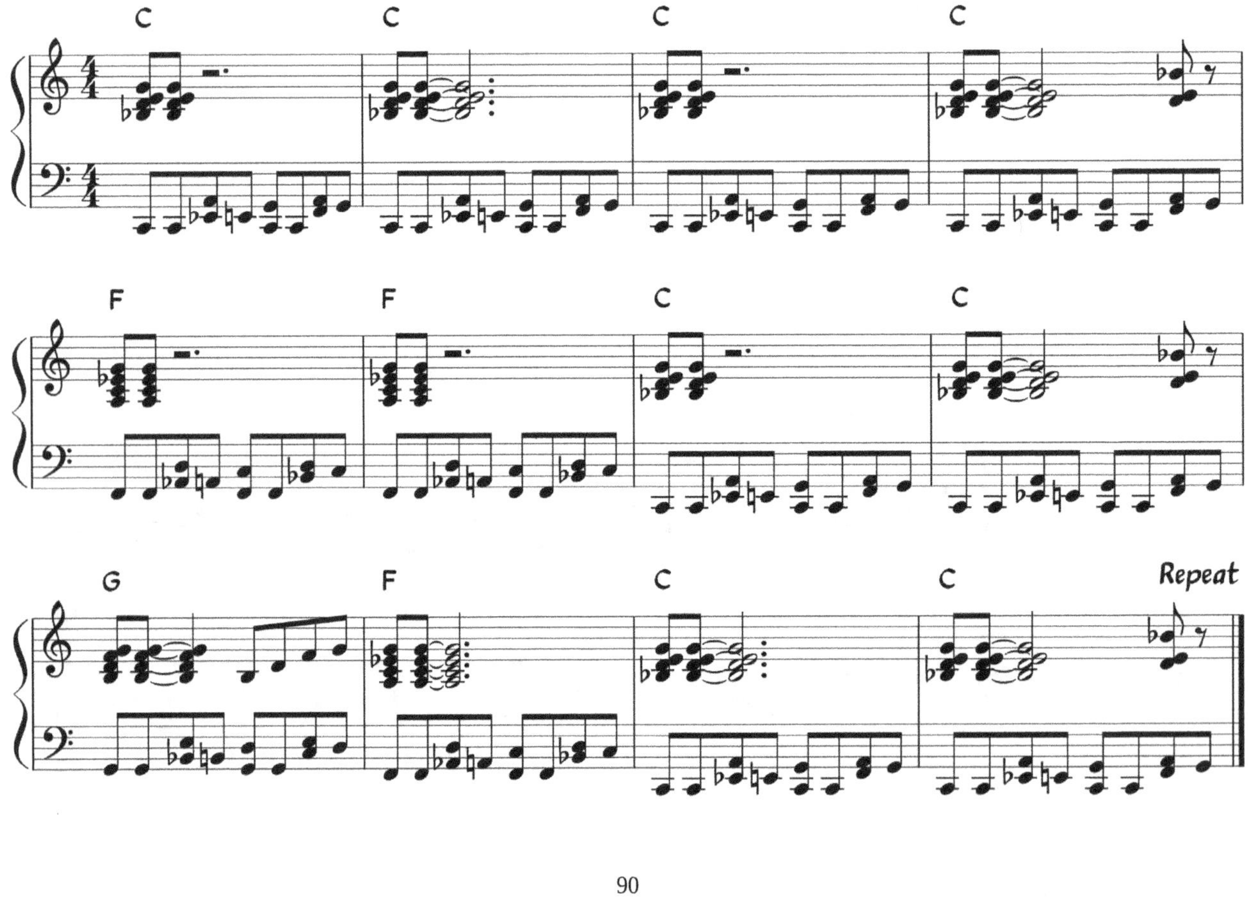

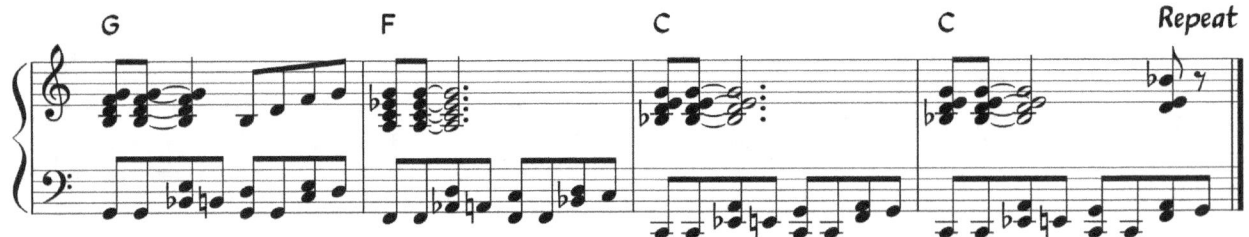

Five Note Chords

Although the number of notes used within a chord tends to be a maximum of four, it's possible – be it in limited situations – to play a five fingered chord.

Admittedly, generally speaking this sounds like quite a bad idea, and I'd agree. Too many notes can sound muddy together not to mention the issues with placing all five digits on keys at the same time, but it can work quite nicely in limited circumstances. We aren't talking about any random chord but more specifically discussing a form of sixth chord.

Five Note 'C6' Chord (With Fingering Numbers)

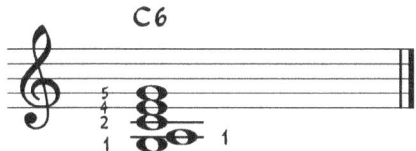

The chord '**C6**' chord above differs from normal in that the fifth has been repeated on the bottom. The fingering numbers show the bottom two notes are being played by the thumb simultaneously. So you aren't actually using more than the usual four fingers at all.

Other Example Chords

Due to the shape of some chords this isn't possible for every sixth, so in reality it's quite limited but worth knowing. Below are the other sixths laid out in a manner that is playable.

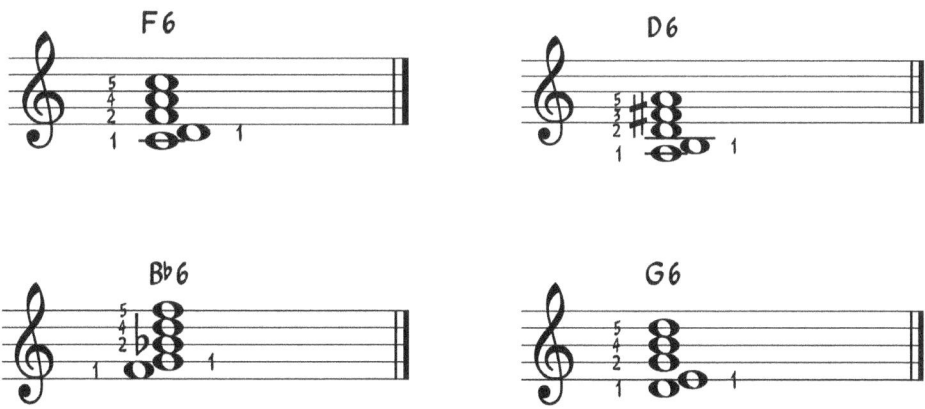

Comping Pattern. 24

Comping Pattern. 25

Comping Pattern. 26

62 AUDIO

Comping Pattern. 27

63 AUDIO

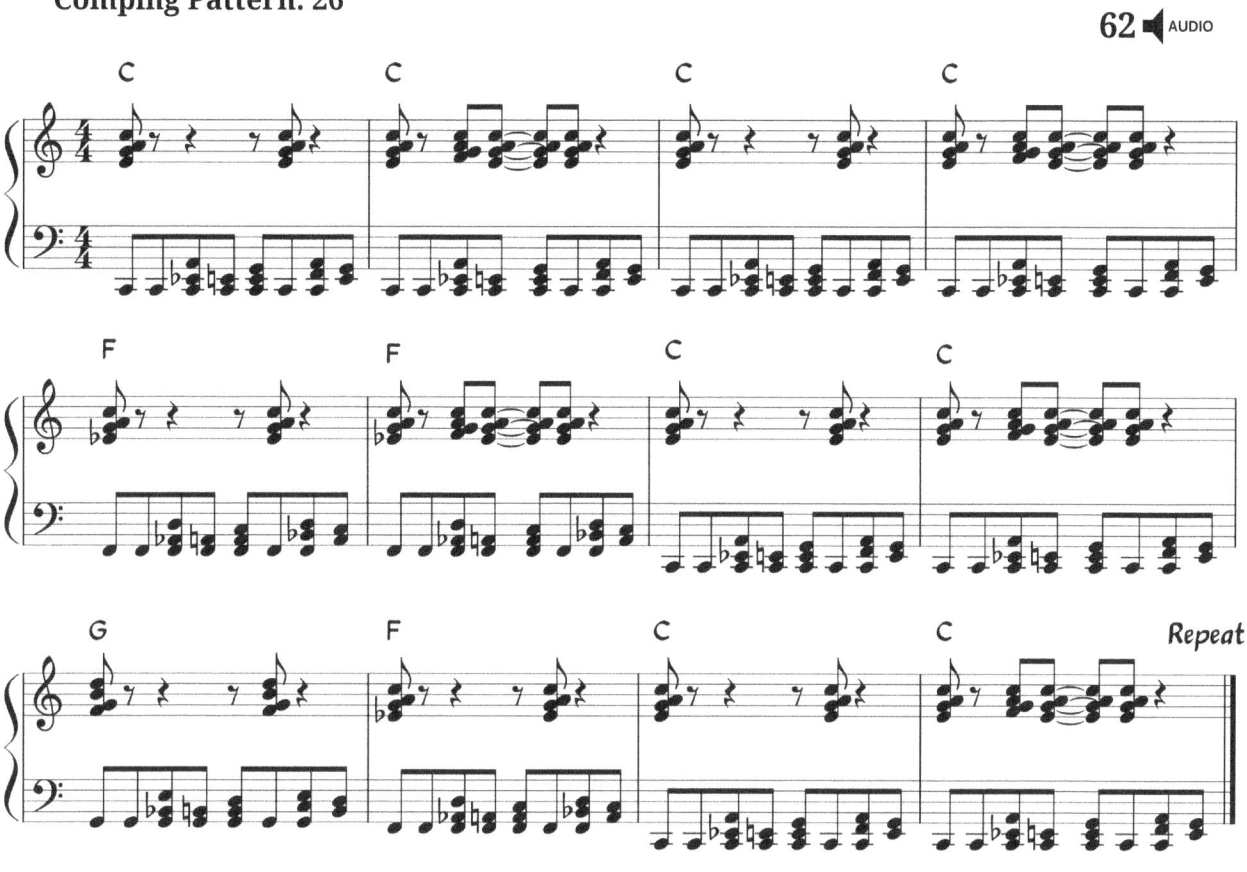

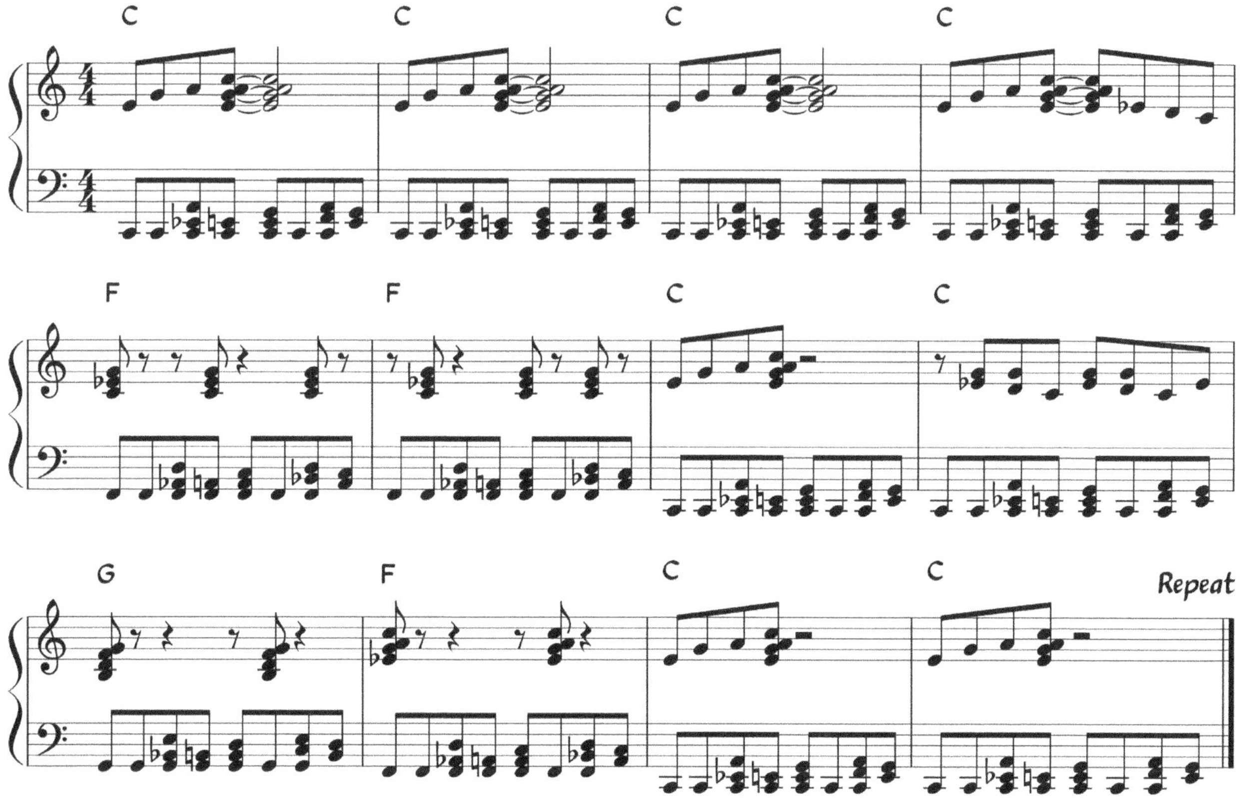

Stompy Toes

Minor Chords

Minor chords aren't something you hear too often in boogie-woogie, but that's not to say you can't slip them in from time to time. Their contrast to the usual major chords is a great sound when used in a certain manner. One of which we can have a look at below.

Used sparingly with the '**I**' chord it can create a something that adds a nice twist. We are going to do this on bar numbers seven and eight, coming in after the '**IV**' chord and leading into the '**V**' chord. You could also use the minor chords on bars eleven and twelve if you wish.

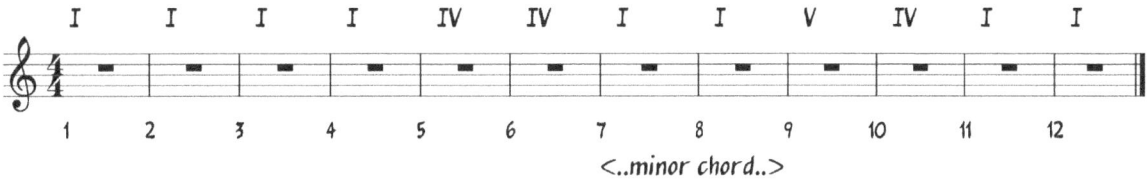

I think it works best with the minor-third at the top of the chord and although the example uses a seventh you could equally use something else. For example, if you played the '**F**' chord as '**F9**' you could carry the chord over without change as it would become a '**Cm6**' and work nicely.

Comping Pattern 28

Walk-Up Patterns

For our purposes the term 'walk-up' is referring to a movement with the left-hand that transitions between chords, normally by moving from one root note to the root of the next chord. I call these 'walk-ups' as you are walking up (although admittedly sometimes down) the keyboard. These are a great way of breaking things up and introducing the chord changes in an interesting manner.

This pattern will start with the root of the currant chord and move through the three notes directly below the root of the target chord. We are moving from 'C' with the target note being the 'F' (being a 'I' to 'IV' chord change).

Walk-Up Notes For 'C' To 'F' Change

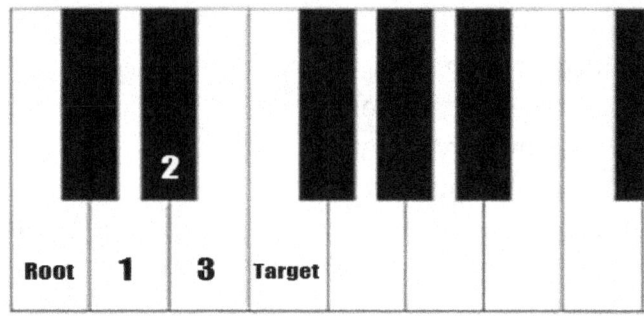

Shown As Notation

Typical 12-bar Example   66 AUDIO

A typical example of this used in a walking-bass style. Starting with the root and passing through the three notes discussed above.

NOTE

Just remember that when you are moving upwards to a new chord, the target root note and the three notes in chromatic order just below it will always work, if you use these then you can't go far wrong.

'C' To 'F' Movement

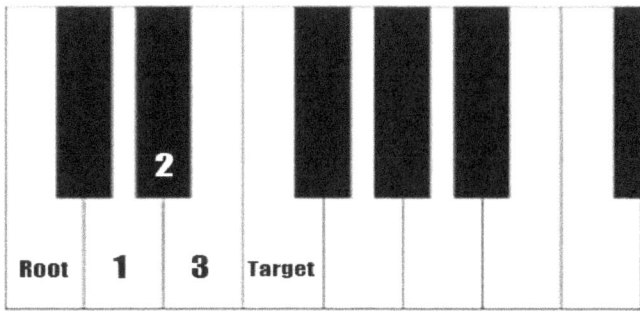

'C' To 'G' Movement

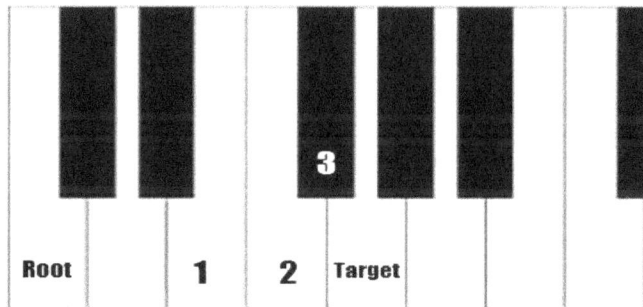

'E♭' To 'A♭' Movement

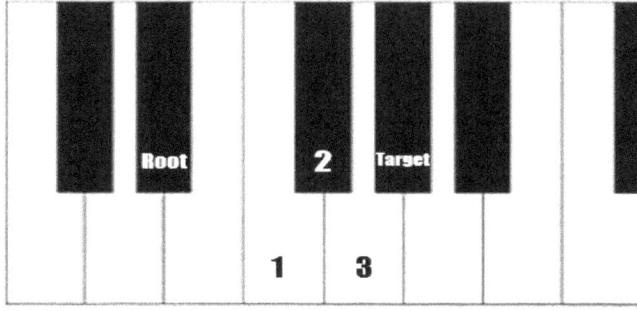

The movement itself can be played in a manner of different ways with single notes, octaves, fifths, or even whole chords if you wish. My personal favourite is the walking-bass style pattern but all of them shown below can work well depending on the context of the song. Single notes are fine within a slower blues context with octaves sounding stronger, perhaps. Experiment with it all and find what you like.

Variety Of Different Options

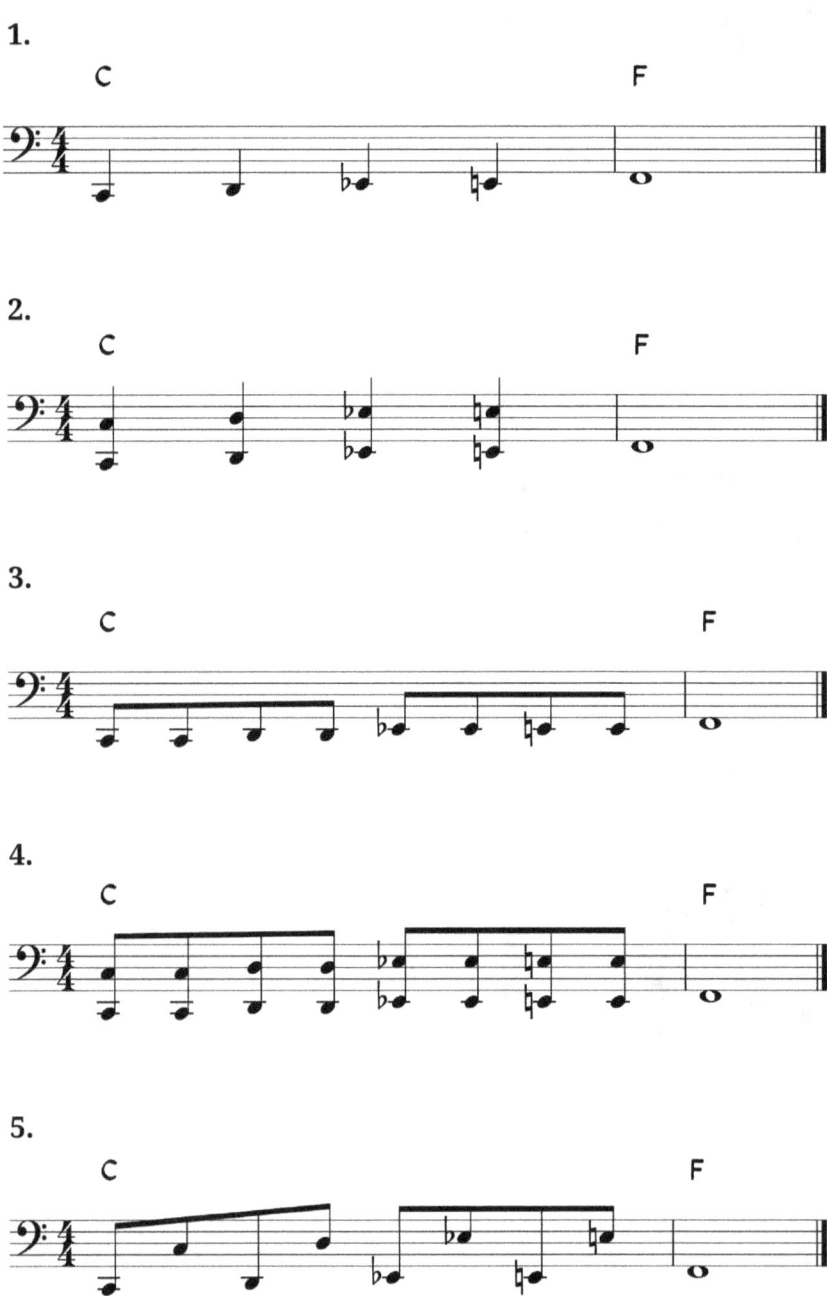

6.

7.

8.

9.

10.

11.

Alternate Timing

Instead of each note being played on the beat you can off-set them to create a different rhythmic feel. Still starting with the root note it now moves on the later half of the first beat and the target chords root note is hit in the preceding bar.

Variety Of Different Options

6.

7.

8.

9.

10.

11.

12-bar Practice Example. 1

12-bar Practice Example. 2

12-bar Practice Example. 3   69 AUDIO

12-bar Practice Example. 4   70 AUDIO

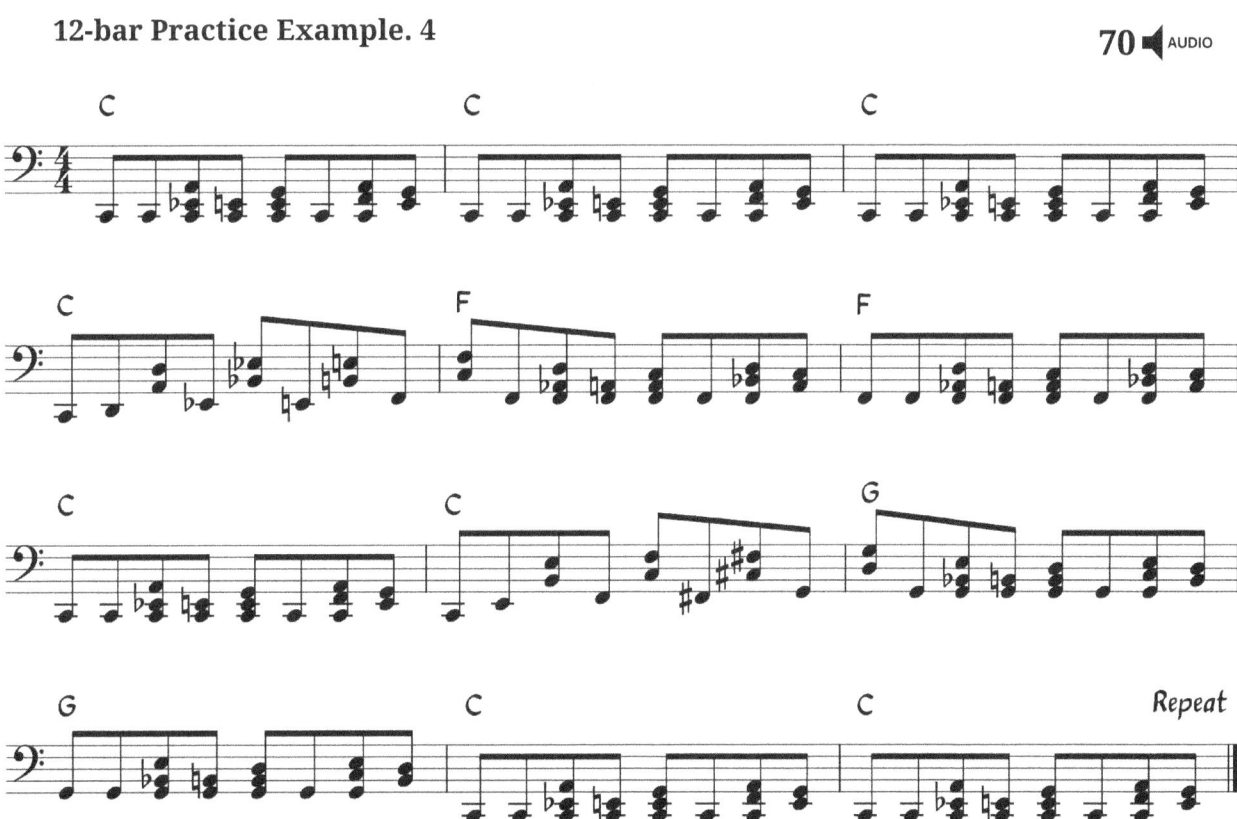

12-bar Practice Example. 5

12-bar Practice Example. 6

12-bar Practice Example. 7

Comping Pattern. 29

Comping Pattern. 30

Comping Pattern. 31

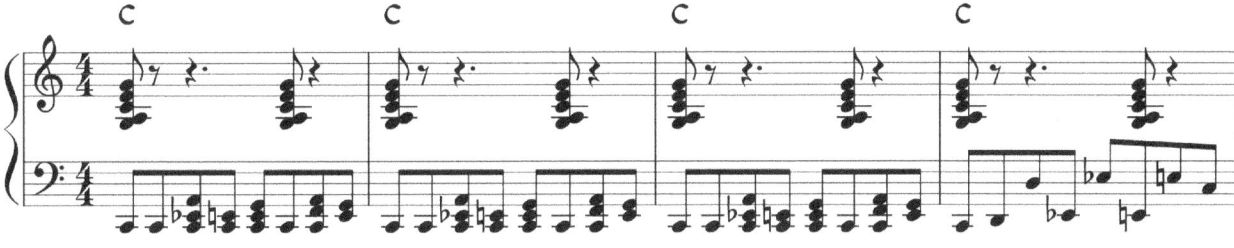

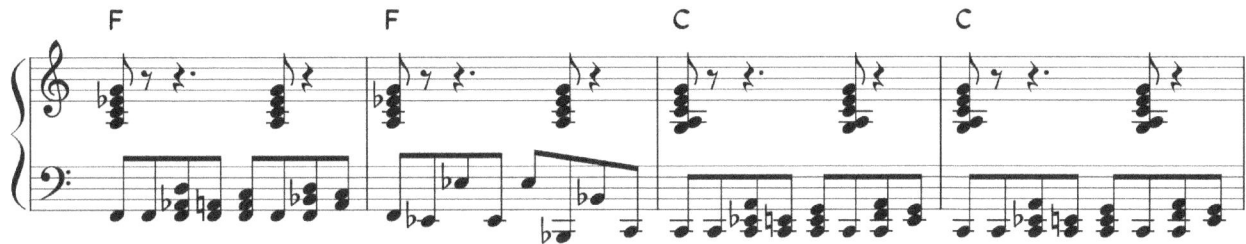

Comping Pattern. 32

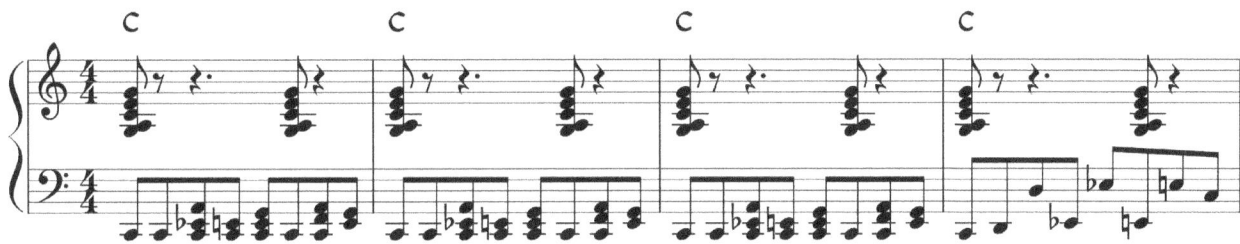

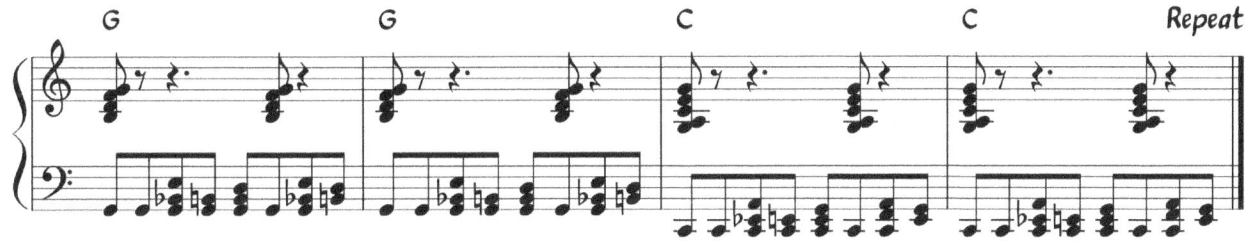

Chopping Walk Boogie

Boogie On The Bank

Left-Hand Pattern 9

This left-hand pattern consists of two bars rather than the usual one and is unusual in that it is a pattern of two parts. The first bar is a typical rhythmic boogie-pattern followed by the second using a walking style, which is similar to the walk-up pattern discussed previously.

The second bars walk-up section moves chromatically upwards through the sixth, flat-seventh and major seventh before reaching the root note.

Have a practice of this with the left-hand alone before moving on to add the right-hand. Start off slowly, gradually build up the tempo as you become accustomed to the pattern.

12-bar Practice Example

A good general technique with the left-hand is to move towards the root of the following chord (at chord changes). This not only sounds good but also makes the transition between chords easy in the physical sense. This works well with this particular pattern.

Example. 1 Standard Walk-Up

Here you have the '**C**' walking up to the '**F**" using the second, flat-third and third (of the original chord).

You can see that the walk-up notes at the end of the example above are the same as used in the basic pattern for the '**F**' chord (as below) hence why it works moving to the '**F**'.

NOTE

Just remember that after the root note the walk-up moves chromatically through the three notes directly below the root of the target chord. Below shows the target note is '**F**' therefore we use the three preceding notes leading up to it.

Walk-Up Target Notes To 'F'

Example. 2 Walk-Up Variation

Moving back down to the '**C**' from the '**F**' we leave out the major-seventh and just use the sixth and flat-seventh (referring to the '**F**' chord).

Movement Notes 'F' to 'C'

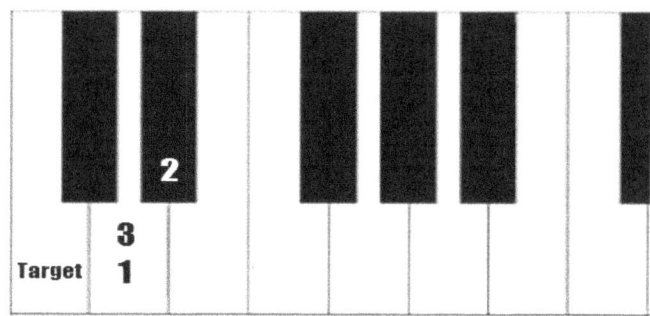

Example. 3   Walk-Up 'C' To 'G'

Moving to the '**G**' chord sees us use the third, fourth and flat-fifth. Again, this is the three notes below the target note.

Walk-Up Notes To Target Note 'G'

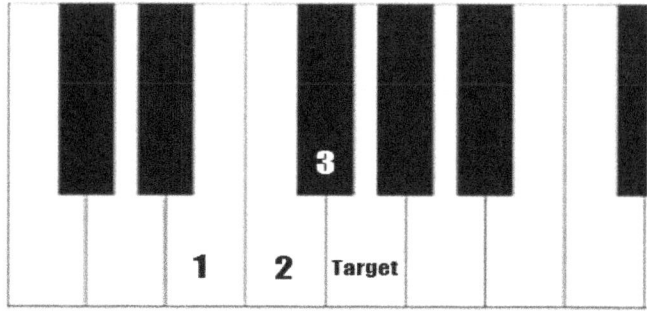

Example. 4 Walk-Down Variation

Here we have a walk down using the seventh, sixth and fifth.

Movement Notes 'G' to 'C'

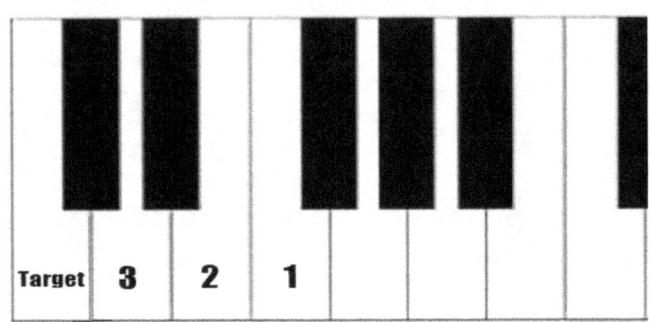

12-bar Practice Example. 1

81 AUDIO

Alternative. 1

An alternative for moving from '**G**' to '**C**' could be something like this. Using the sharp-five and flat-third of the '**G**' chord. Alternatively, think of it as the flat-third and seventh of the target chord '**C**'.

Movement Notes 'G' to 'C'

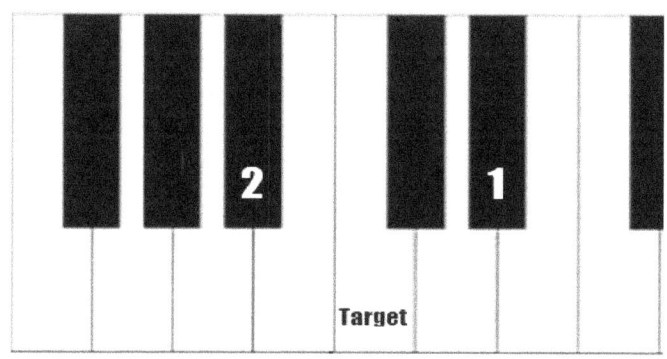

12-bar Practice Example. 2

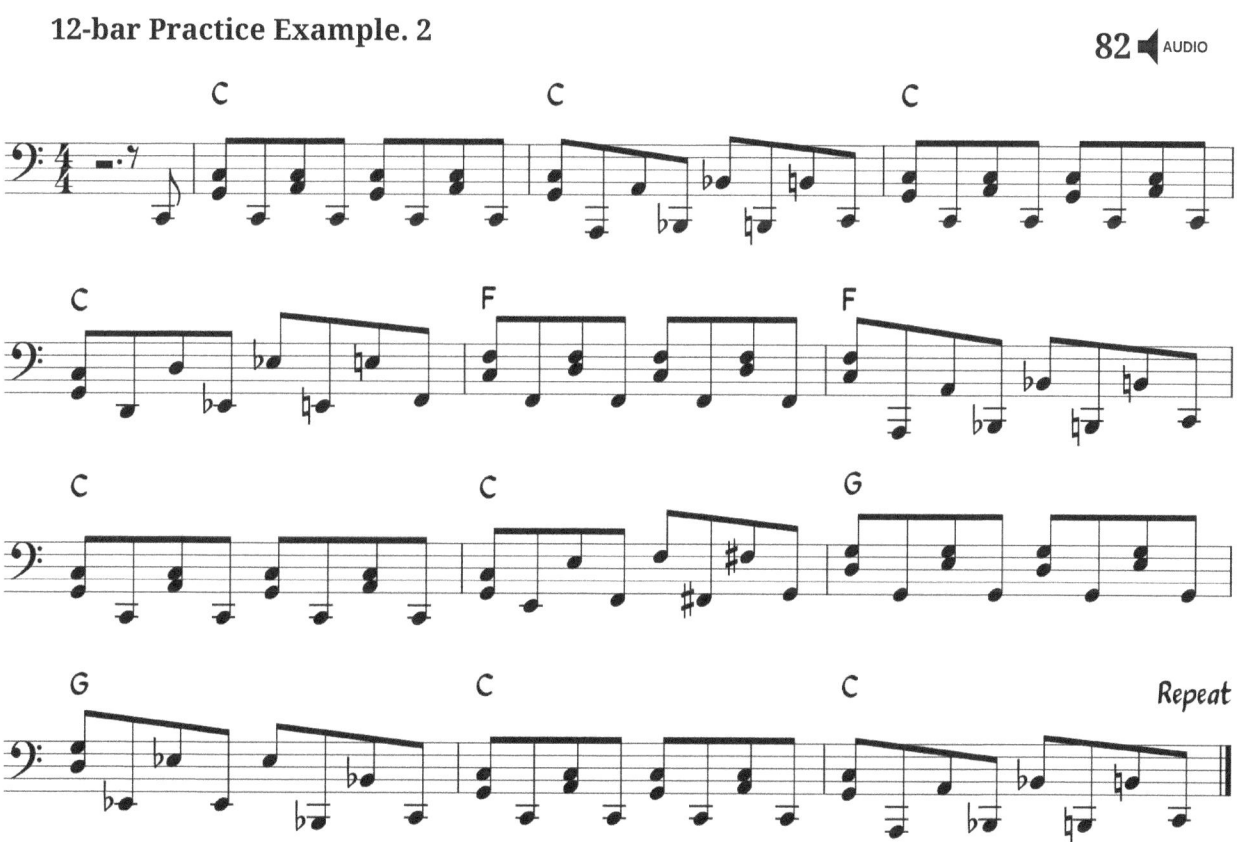

Alternatives Using The IV Chord

If you wanted to use the 'IV' chord in bar ten instead of having two bars of the 'V' chord, here are a few options that you could try out.

Option. 1

Option. 2

Option. 3

Option. 4

Busy Bass Boogie

Playing In Other Keys

Up to this point we have only been using the key of '**C**' and as nice as that is on the piano there are of course more keys available. As you no doubt realise, there are twelve keys to consider (discounting duplicates like F#/G♭ or A#/B♭) so what should you look at if going beyond the key of '**C**'.

There are several important aspects to discuss here.

1. Do you need to worry about **every** key

2. How to play a riff in a different key (transposing)

3. How best to practice when there are so many keys

Over the next few pages we will look at all of these points which will hopefully allow you to think about what *you* personally want to do and so what to be concentrating on (this will be different for everybody). We will also show how to transpose a simple pattern into another key and discuss ideas on how to practise over different keys (along with practise in general).

NOTE

Moving on with the book (later volumes in the series) we shall be introducing examples in other keys. Starting with '**C**' is a good idea, as it makes any explanations easier to understand and also easier when first playing to get a handle on the mechanics of it all. But it's important to later branch out as different keys have a different sound, plus some things suit different keys better than others, not to mention it just pushes you further as a musician.

Do You Need All The Keys

Warning, we are going to use the word 'twelve a lot here'. There are twelve keys that you can play boogie-woogie in (dismissing overlapping sharps and flats). Twelve different ways you can play every left-hand bass pattern, twelve different ways you can play every right-hand riff. Twelve different versions of each scale, twelve different versions of everything you might learn and so twelve combinations of notes you need to learn just to play the exact same thing. When you stop and think about it, that is an awful lot to learn and if we come down to reality it's not a realistic proposition for most people. So if you are a mere mortal and don't have an eternity to practice (like most) what should you do?

What do you want to do?

Ask yourself a question, what do you want from this? What is it you aim to do by learning this style of music? Do you want to be the next Axel Zwingenberger or Jools Holland? Do you want to earn a living from music? Or are you just learning because you like the music and it's fun to play? The answer to this makes a big difference.

Serious Aspirations?

If you do have serious aspirations towards a career playing boogie-woogie piano, then yes, you will need to be-able to play in more than just good old '**C**'. Some keys are certainly used more than others that's without doubt, and you might well concentrate on them more than the slightly more obscure keys, for instance you might hear '**G**' being used more often then '**A♭**'. But an ability to play/improvise in any key would be advisable and desirable for a couple of reasons.

1.

For one, it helps when playing with other people. If you're in a band setting then you can end up playing in all sorts of keys in order to suit the other musicians (which can be annoying at times, but that's life). Remember that '**C**' might be great on the piano but not all instruments are set out the same with different keys suiting other instruments better.

Also, if you have a singer/vocalist then you will probably need to play in a key that will suit their voice. Another point, playing in different keys helps give songs a different sound from each-other. If every song you played was in the same key it could start to sound a little bland after a while in comparison to using different keys.

An important point to make here though is that although the ability to play in all keys is highly desirable, that doesn't mean you have to be an absolute *master* in each and every key. To be-able to play everything equally well in all twelve keys is quite a task and in truth, how many musicians are one-hundred percent at the same standard in all of them? They might be close, but if they are completely honest? As long as you can play to a certain standard in the more obscure keys, then that's probably good enough for most.

2.

Another benefit of learning to improvise in many keys is that it is good for the music. When you change the key, it alters the sound, and you will notice that some patterns/riffs that sounded great in one key, once transposed just don't sound the same, perhaps even to the point of being unusable. But it also works in reverse, allowing you to come up with something new in a different key that you wouldn't have done previously.

The physical keys used are different in different keys, and as the layout of the keyboard has white keys broken up by black keys, the same scale in a different key can create different patterns in the physical sense. (The shape/movement required of your fingers/hands). This can be a good and bad thing as you will find that a riff that's a joy to play in one key just doesn't work nicely in a another key due to the keyboard layout. The flip-side of this of course is that when improvising in another key you can come up with something that just wouldn't of occurred to you in your usual go to key. Change can do you good, so they say, or at least sometimes anyway.

Just For The Fun Of It?

I would imagine the vast majority of people who pick up an instrument (I wouldn't recommend literally picking up a piano, they're quite heavy) do so just for the sheer enjoyment of learning and playing music. After all, there are far easier ways to make a living in this world – so if this is the case, does this change things for you?

Well I'd say both yes and no, but mainly yes, maybe.

If you are learning boogie-woogie just because you enjoy it and have no aspirations to playing it professionally/semi-professionally, then I would most definitely say not to obsess too much about all the keys. Some people might disagree with this, but stop and think about it. It takes a lot of work to learn an instrument, period, it takes even longer to learn a style of music well enough to actually improvise within it. So, to learn everything you know in every key will take even more time and even more work. This is fine if you have that time free and the inclination to spend that time on the piano (and it will take an awful lot of time). But the vast majority of people have other jobs, hobbies, families, and simply don't have the option to spend *that* much time on an instrument. Maybe they wouldn't even want to spend *that* long practising all the time (too much can certainly take the fun out of it).

If this is you, then I would recommend learning the most commonly used keys first. You can look at the other keys at a later date when you have a feel for the music and can improvise okay in a few keys. '**C**' is the obvious first port of call, followed perhaps by '**G**' and then maybe '**F**'. You will come across a lot of sheet music in these keys and they suit the piano keyboard quite well. You will come across sheet music that has songs in other keys, and this is a great way to start learning new keys without actually thinking about it, as you are simply copying what's on the page. This of course will create a degree of muscle memory of patterns within that key without you even realising, so when you do look at improvising in that key you will already have a bit of a feel of it over the keyboard.

Now, that all said, just because you are playing just for fun (perhaps with limited time) there's no need to think limited. You can still work to learn to play in the other keys, I'd recommend it even, and you can still reach a high standard it's just that it will take longer. This can be considered a long term goal, improving at anything you do as a hobby is a long term goal, in time you will improve, but the difference is that you aren't in any rush. Don't worry about learning it all at once, take your time, concentrate on a few keys to start with and then add another at a later date, if you want to and feel ready. You can improve at your own speed, and ultimately it doesn't matter what destination you reach on your journey because it's all about the journey. It's about enjoying the learning process, enjoying discovering new things, the joy of seeing yourself learn something that you couldn't previously do, hearing something new come alive on the piano and mostly just enjoying the music.

To Summarise

If you're happy just playing in a few keys for your own enjoyment, then there's nothing wrong with that at all. Just remember, you're not trying to pass a test, there's no award, prize for learning another key, so take it as far as you wish, learn them all over time or just a few, it's up to you.

In short there is no right or wrong answer, just do what's best for you personally, whatever you are happy with.

Transposing

You might be used to doing this kind of thing but if it's new to you then don't worry, it's not a big deal when it comes down to it. The idea and practice is quite simple, but of course to do this quickly takes practice (like everything). Fortunately we aren't talking about transposing entire songs but rather short patterns or riffs that you wish to memorise in other keys to enable you to build up a database to use when improvising.

You could of course use software to transpose even a simple one bar pattern, although I would advise just practising doing this in your head and on the keyboard instead. Ultimately, what you do/work out by yourself will stay with you far more effectively than something you just read on a page or from a computer screen.

Example. 1

Let's look at a bass-line from earlier in the book. It is written along with the interval numbers, which shows that it uses the first, fifth, and sixth degrees of the '**C**' major scale. Knowing the original key of the riff and knowing the intervals that create it gives us all the information we need to move it into another key. Knowing the intervals isn't one hundred percent required mind you, but it helps.

So, what next...?

Different Method Options

1. Moving up/down keyboard visually

2. Use knowledge of scales to recreate the pattern

3. Use a piece of software to do the work for you

1.   **Moving up/down keyboard visually**

This is a perfectly viable option if theory is not your thing. There's nothing wrong with that at all, many truly great musicians aren't great with music theory, and this would no doubt have included plenty of the original boogie-woogie pianists (and current ones for that matter).

Chopping Bass Pattern

Here we have the notes used for the chopping bass pattern in the key of '**C**' shown on the keyboard using the numbers of the intervals as reference.

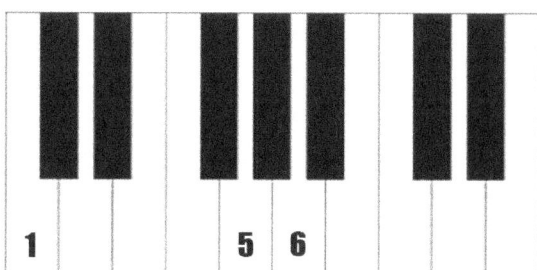

So if you want to know this pattern in another key (we'll choose '**F**' as the example) we have to move all the notes up the keyboard but keep them in the same order. So if we count the keys chromatically starting from '**C**' and move up to the '**F**' we will count five semi-tones.

Count Up From 'C' To 'F'

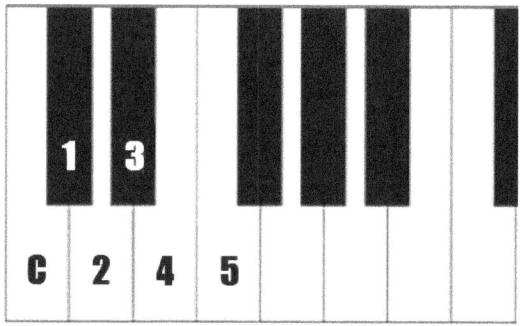

Knowing that the '**F**' is five semi-tones higher than the '**C**' means it is then easy to move any note from a pattern/riff played in '**C**' to the new key of '**F**'.

C – Becomes – F

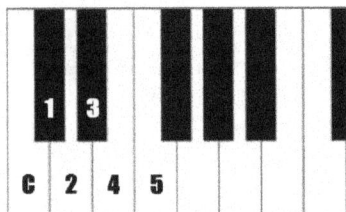

G – Becomes – C

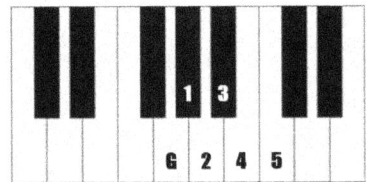

A – Becomes – D

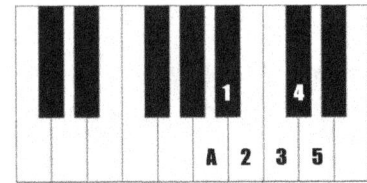

Pattern Notes Transposed To New Key Of 'F'

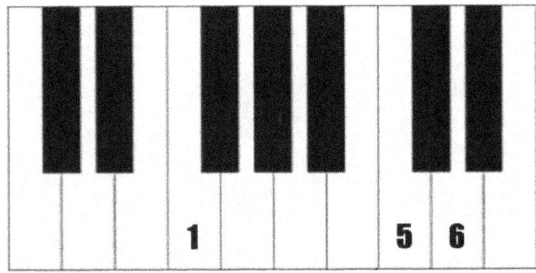

You can apply the same idea to any riff, pattern, or key change, all you need to know is how many semi-tones you need to move, which is as simple as counting the keys between the two relative notes.

C To D   Two semi-tones

To move a pattern from the key of '**C**' to '**D**' means you have to move every note within the pattern up just two semi-tones/notes on the keyboard.

C To G   Seven semi-tones

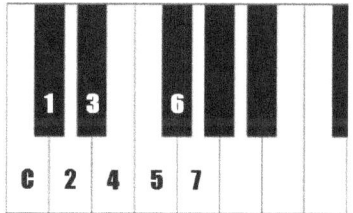

To move a pattern from the key of '**C**' to '**G**' means you have to move every note within the pattern up seven semi-tones/notes on the keyboard.

> **NOTE**
> Obviously this works easily with simple patterns like the left-hand in the example, although with some of the more complex riffs you might learn, it becomes more involved and possibly confusing. (With so much more going on). It still works perfectly well, just take it one note at a time, and it will all fall into place.

2. Using knowledge of scales to recreate the pattern

This requires you to know your major scales well, or at least the ones that relate to the keys you wish to transpose to. If you know these or learn them then this is probably a faster way of working, although the end result is the same.

'C' Major Scale

The 'C' major scale is shown below (treble clef) with the notes and interval numbers displayed. You can clearly see which note corresponds to the scale intervals (The 2nd is 'D' and the 5th is 'G' etc).

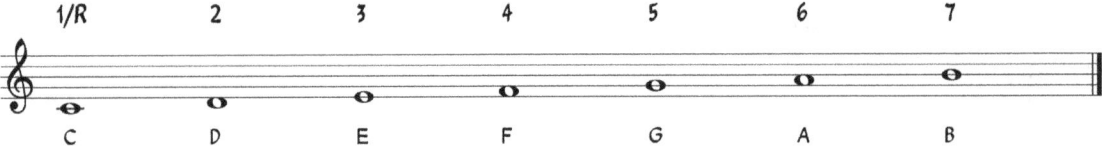

Notes Used Within Chopping Style Bass Pattern

Taking the same chopping style bass pattern again we can see all the notes from the riff highlighted within the major scale shown below.

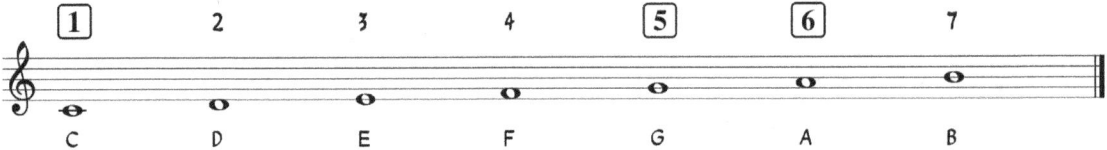

Now we know the degrees of the 'C' major scale used for the pattern, if we go to a new key we can use the equivalent degrees of the new scale to create the same pattern within the new key.

This is obviously a more efficient way of approaching this, but it depends on how well you know the makeup of the scales. Ultimately whatever works for you is fine, but it just proves that knowing those scales is always a good thing.

Example Change (New Key 'E')

The pattern we transpose uses the root, fifth and sixth, you can look at the scale of the new key and see what the same intervals correspond to. The relevant intervals are highlighted and so revealing the notes required to create the pattern.

Pattern Intervals

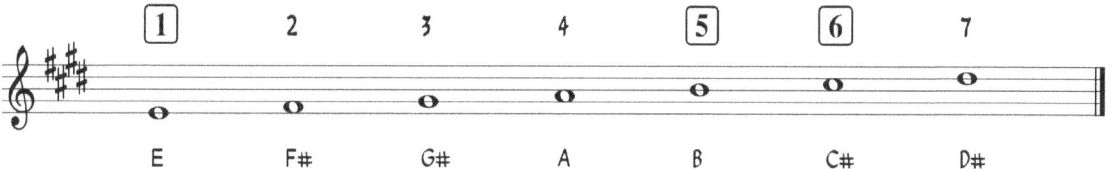

Chopping Pattern In Key Of 'E'

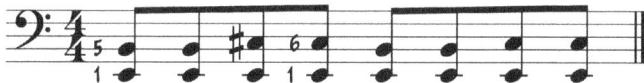

Example Change (New Key 'G')

Here we are changing the pattern into the key of '**G**'. Using the same intervals from the relevant major scale below. The relevant intervals are highlighted and so revealing the notes required to create the same pattern.

Pattern Intervals

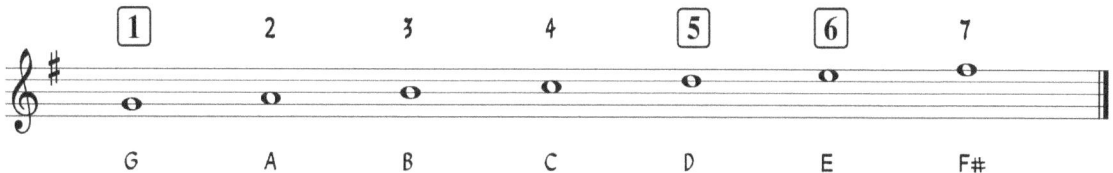

Chopping Pattern In Key Of 'G'

3. Use a piece of software to do the work for you

This is certainly an option if you wish. You could use any type of scoring software, which could be a Daw/Sequencer with a score page or purpose made scoring software. Simply play the pattern/riff in question or enter the notes manually and then click on whatever menu you need to transpose the music up or down to your desired key.

Personally I wouldn't recommend this sort of approach as it stifles your own progress. If you aren't familiar with transposing music to different keys, then this may seem an easier option, but then that is an issue. If you let a PC do all the work for you, then you'll never improve at doing it yourself and develop that skill.

Entire Songs

The exception would be when it comes to transposing large sections or even entire songs. The amount of work involved here means it might make sense to use software instead. Although it wouldn't be very often you would even need to do this is in reality. Sheet music you buy be in various keys, and you'd learn them without thought of changing the key. The only time you might need to would be in a band setting where the key doesn't suit the other musicians/singer, that may or may-not be an issue for you.

Practising In Other Keys

Once you know how to go about transposing a riff into other keys, what is the best way to go about practising something in all the different keys?

If you want to practice an individual riff/pattern then you have a couple of ways to approach it.

1. Practice the riff systematically in each key

By this I mean that you should take the pattern you are working on and play it systematically through each and every key. There are different ways that you could approach this, but ultimately it amounts to the same thing, repeating the pattern over and over and over again! It sounds monotonous, and it probably is, but it's repetition that makes you learn.

2. Practice the riff over a progression in each key

Here we could take the riff and practise it in a real setting, playing it with both hands in some form of twelve-bar progression. It doesn't have to be anything special, just something to turn it into a real piece of music instead of a mindless repetitive exercise.

Pros - Cons

The first option is far quicker. You can run through as many keys as you wish in relatively quick fashion with nothing else to distract you. The downside is that it might well feel mindlessly monotonous and put you off from practising at all.

The second option makes the practise far more interesting and potentially enjoyable, not to mention that you can practice using the pattern in question with different combinations of left and right-hands. The downside of this though is that it will take far longer to move through a number of different keys.

Method One

As discussed, this will entail you playing the riff/pattern in question in each key, starting with 'C' and moving up the keyboard one key/semi-tone at a time. You can of course start on any key you wish, but 'C' or perhaps 'A' would be the most obvious choices.

Piano Keyboard Practice Order

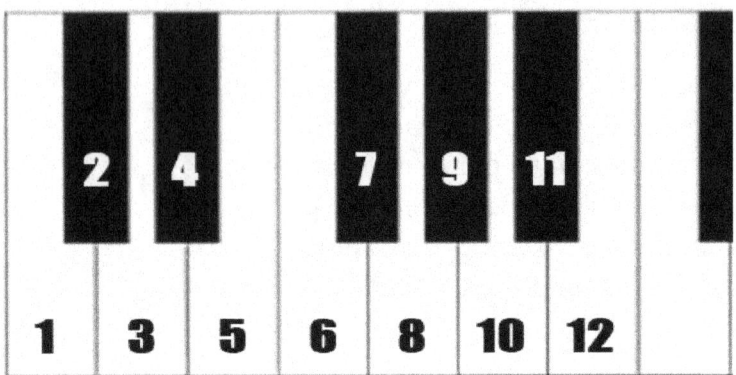

How Many Repetitions

How many times you will want to play the pattern in each key is entirely up to you, but I would probably suggest **ten**. It's a nice round number and gives enough repetitions for it to make an impressionism on your brain but without being too many times that it will drive you insane with boredom. You don't have to stick to this number, but it is a good starting point (see the point below).

Important Note

A point I will make is this, too many repetitions at one time of the same thing can be counterproductive. The first ten repetitions might force you to think about what you're playing, but once the pattern becomes comfortable you will go into a sort of autopilot mode, and will no longer be challenging yourself and using the brain. At this point it's no-longer having so much effect, time to swap keys. By the time you have gone through all the keys and return to the first you, will need to force yourself to think yet again. This is more effective, repetition is how we learn but keep rotating the subject matter.

Alternative Order Of Practise

You could use an alternative order of practising through the keys. Instead of moving up the keyboard one key/semi-tone at a time you could practice the pattern by going through the circle of fifths.

The Circle Of Fifths

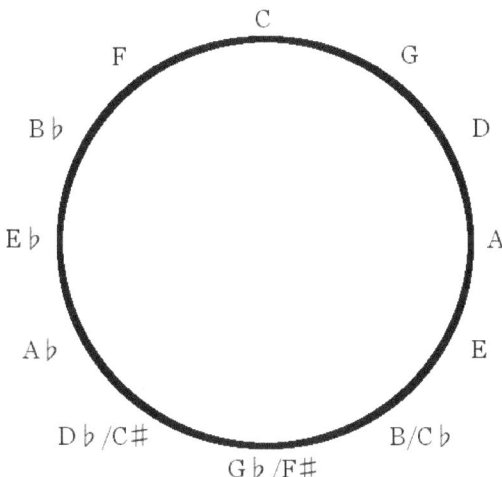

We won't go into much detail regarding the circle of fifths as such (you may know all about it, but if not a theory book or internet search will fill you in properly) but if you move around the circle clockwise you will see that each key is a fifth higher than the preceding one (seven semi-tones higher).

Why is this useful to us?

Well it might be useful because it will move through the different keys in the order of how many accidentals (sharps/flats) they have, increasing each time.

C = 0
G = 1
D = 2
A = 3
E = 4
B = 5
F♯ = 6

And then it moves in the reverse order of how many flats there are in each key, decreasing the number of accidentals until it goes back to zero.

G♭ = 6
D♭ = 5
A♭ = 4
E♭ = 3
B♭ = 2
F = 1
C = 0

Practising a pattern through the circle of fifths might appeal to you because of the gradual increase and then decrease in accidentals. Generally speaking, the more accidentals the more challenging it can be to play, so with this method you start off with the more simplistic key (no accidentals) and gradually move through them, increasing the number by one at a time. (And its potential difficultly level). Once you reach the maximum number it moves the other direction and decreases the number through the flat keys.

Piano Keyboard Practice Order

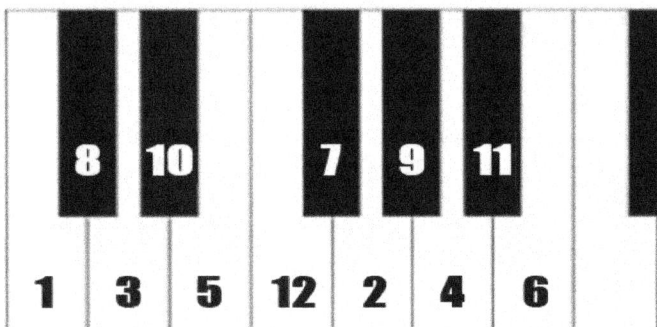

Method Two

This method consists of practising the riff/pattern by using it in a real context like playing it over a twelve-bar progression. This has some advantages.

1. **Left-hand In Realistic Setting**

When practising the left-hand it might help to play it in a real setting along with the chord changes that you would be using in an actual piece of music. This also helps to get those chord changes ingrained on your brain for automatic recall.

2. **Right-hand Over Left-hand**

It is one thing learning to play a pattern on an individual basis, but what about when you go to play it with the other hand? By practising with both it helps put the two together as you're working on left/right-hand independence at the same time as practising specific riffs/patterns.

Which Version?

Which method you prefer is up to you, both have advantages but what I will say is that the first method (single hand) is probably best initially while the pattern is more challenging but once you are able to play it effectively, then the second method becomes more viable and possibly more enjoyable, and if it's more enjoyable, then anybody and everybody is more likely to actually do it. But ultimately a combination of both ideas is probably most effective.

IMPROVISING
BOOGIE-WOOGIE

Volume Two

Left-Hand Pattern 1

The type of patterns we are beginning with here are in a style that's perhaps a little Yancey like. They have a nice, slightly laid back feel compared to the usual frenetic boogie patterns. The two examples below can be combined as you feel fitting.

1.

2.

It is only using the root, third and fifth, so is technically quite simple, although it will still need practice to combine with the right-hand.

12-bar Practice Example

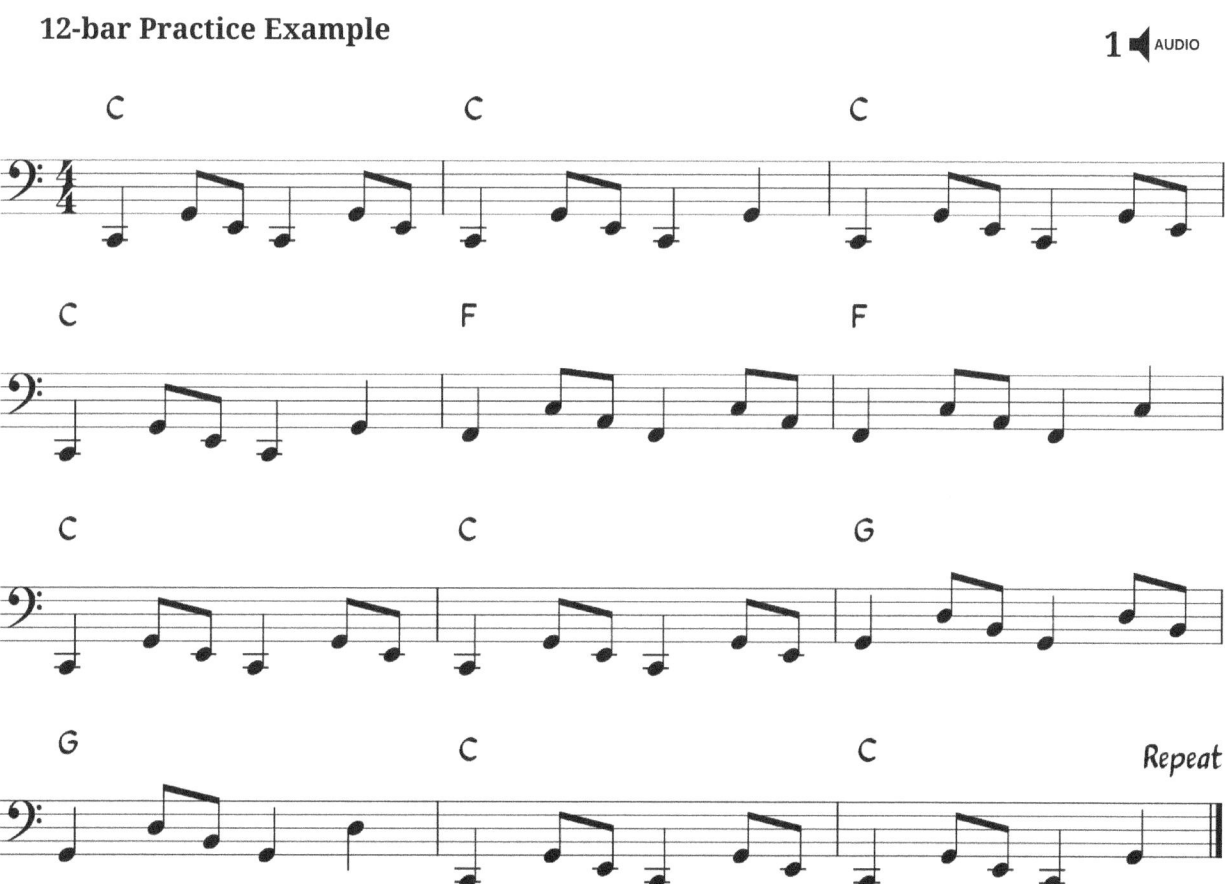

Laid Back Boogie

The Tremolo

What Is A Tremolo?

They could be described as a group of notes that are played in an alternating manner, this can be two notes or an entire chord. Tremolos are used a lot in boogie-woogie and while they are simple enough in theory it can take a little practice to play them smoothly, especially for a longer duration. There are two ways you might see these notated.

Method One

Here each note has been written out individually, which in this example would see you play the 'C' and 'E' alternately at a reasonable fast speed.

Method Two

Here we are using the tremolo symbol to imply how the notes shown should be played. This is exactly the same as the notes shown in method one.,

Tremolo Speed

The speed of the tremolo (or the duration of each note within) is determined by the number of lines within the tremolo sign. The example above used the middle one, 32nd notes.

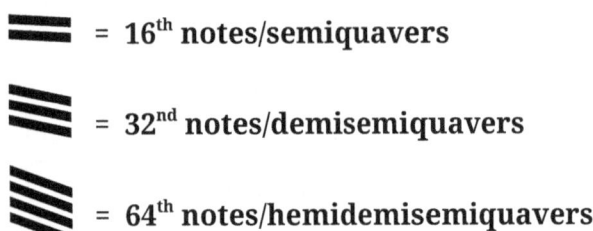

The commonly used tremolo seems to be the 32nd notes type. 16th is a little slow to be effective and 64th would be crazy fast at the sort of tempo boogie-woogie is generally played.

Three Note Chord

Or written in full...

Four Note Chord

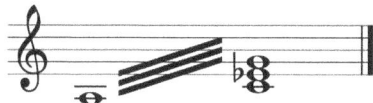

Or written in full...

An important thing to remember when playing these, is to not only use your fingers (especially with the chords) but rather concentrate on using your wrist. The tremolo is split into two halves (a top and a bottom half) so you want to rock your hand from side to side slightly as you move from the bottom notes to the top notes. It's a subtle movement, but it is smoother this way and places far less stress on your fingers.

> Please remember that the amount of notes and their duration is approximate, don't consider trying to make every single note perfectly timed. Instead, just think of it as a rough indication of the speed in which you alternate between them. Basically, don't be fussy here, just knock some notes out, it's more like a wall of sound than anything too precise.

Trem o'clock

Left-Hand Pattern 2

I like this pattern myself, and for some reason it reminds me a little of the music from old western films. Mind you, this ain't no country and western, so don't worry, you haven't got the wrong book by mistake.

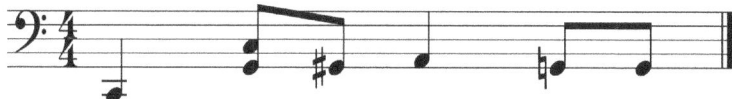

This uses the root, fifth, flat-six and sixth, along with the additional root note an octave higher.

This is one of those boogie patterns that creates more of a relaxed feel and so best at a slightly slower tempo than the more usual aggressive styles. It makes a nice change and is fun to play around with. The following examples use two bars of the '**V**' chord, you can of course use the '**IV**' chord instead on bar ten.

12-bar Practice Example

Pattern Variations

Like every pattern there are numerous ways to vary it slightly, this can be for entire songs or for mixing things up for a bar or two, especially at chord changes.

1.

2.

3.

Combination Example

Wild-West Boogie

Left-Hand Pattern 3

This pattern gives a nod to the likes of Mr Yancey or Meade Lux Lewis. It also has a kind of relaxed feel, although it can be played at a reasonable pace. It's quite infectious.

This pattern uses the root, third and fifth, along with an additional root note an octave higher.

12-bar Practice Example

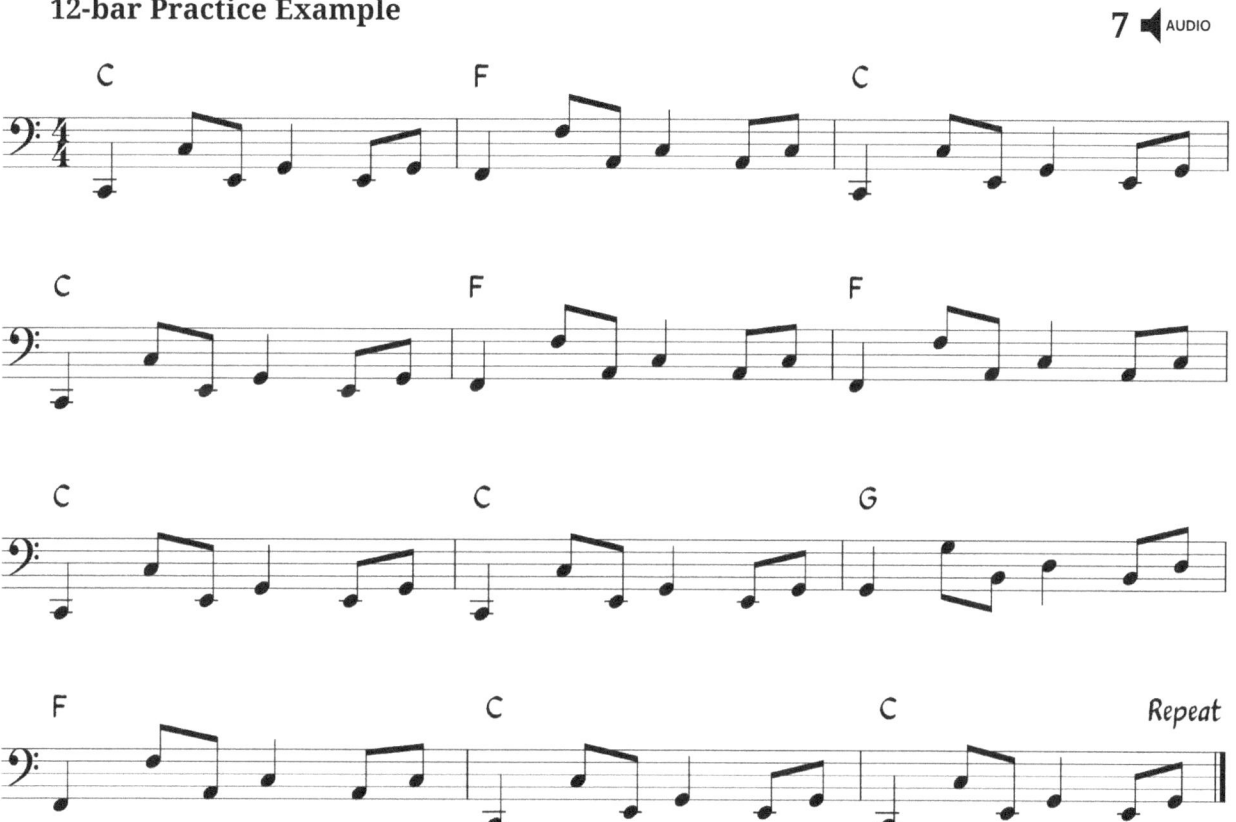

Alternative Timing

The first note on beat two can be played shorter (one triplet duration instead of two) which gives it a slight jumpy-ness, although the difference is not major. Either way is fine.

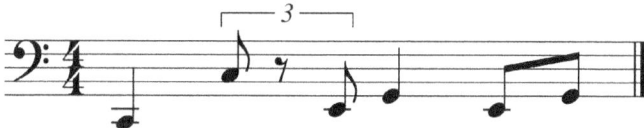

Boogie Fever

Pattern Variations

Here we take a look at a number of different ways you could modify the pattern and create something new. Some are closer to the original than others.

Alternative. 1

Alternative. 2

Alternative. 3

Alternative. 4

Alternative. 5

Alternative. 6

Alternative. 7

Alternative. 8

Alternative. 9

Alternative. 10

Pattern Variations

Playing through these will help give you a feel of where on the keyboard you can go and what works and what doesn't and maybe create a variation of your own.

Alternative. 11

Alternative. 12

Alternative. 13

Alternative. 14

Alternative. 15

Alternative. 16

Alternative. 17

Alternative. 18

Alternative. 19

Alternative. 20

Practice Twelve Bar. 1

Practice Twelve Bar. 2

Practice Twelve Bar. 3

11 AUDIO

Practice Twelve Bar. 4

12 AUDIO

Practice Twelve Bar. 5

Practice Twelve Bar. 6

Practice Twelve Bar. 7　　15 AUDIO

Practice Twelve Bar. 8　　16 AUDIO

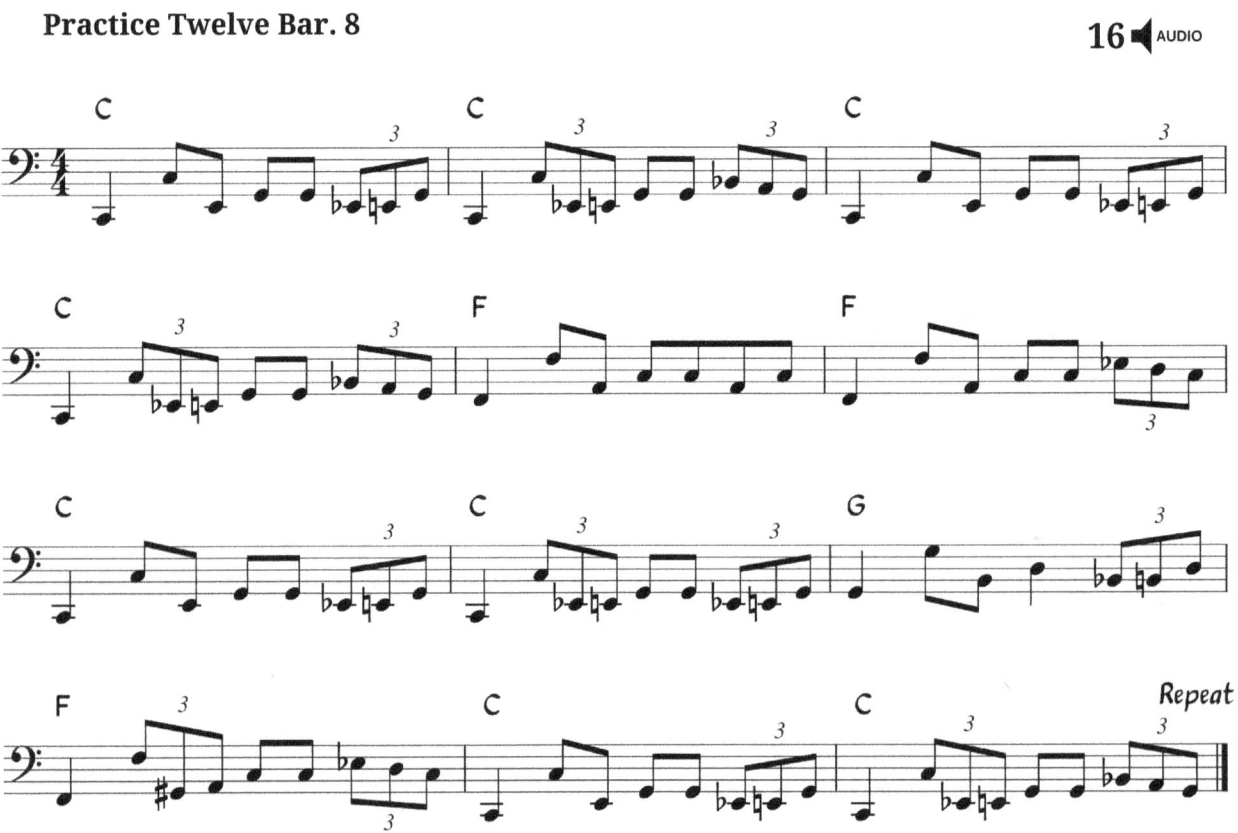

Practice Twelve Bar. 9

Practice Twelve Bar. 10

Practice Twelve Bar. 11

Practice Twelve Bar. 12

Practice Twelve Bar. 13   21 AUDIO

Practice Twelve Bar. 14   22 AUDIO

Windy Boogie

Rhythmic Triplets

We've already used triplets for various parts before, but we can also make triplets the focal rhythmic point of the entire piece. Think of certain Fats Domino songs, and you will have the idea of the sound.

Triplets played throughout

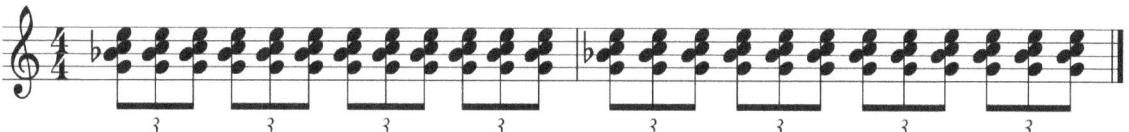

In theory, you could use this over any boogie-woogie left-hand pattern, but it really suits the left-hand we have just been looking at. With the faster more frantic sounding left-hands it sounds far too busy and is physically difficult to play at a very high tempo.

Mixed With Variations

This can of course be mixed with other patterns to break up any monotony and make it more interesting (advisable).

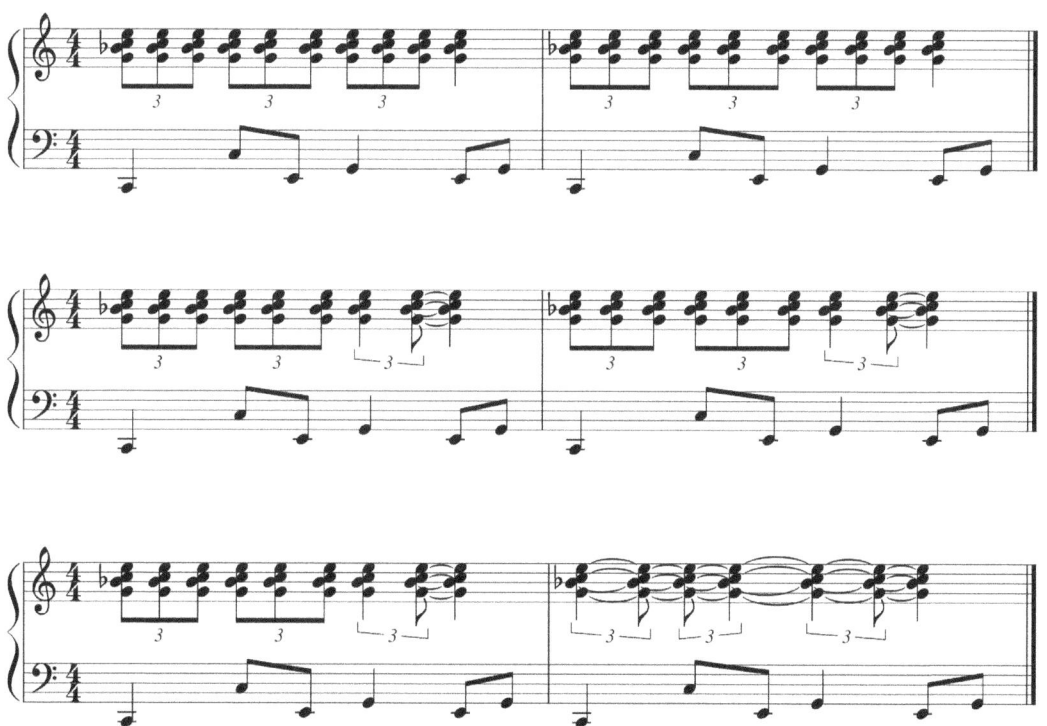

Triplet Comping 1

12-bar Practice Example

Triplet Comping 2

12-bar Practice Example

Triplet Comping 3

12-bar Practice Example

Unusual Timing

In the last song example you might have noticed a couple of bars of what might be considered unusual timing, or at least certainly a contrast to the rest of the piece. By this I am referring to the right-hand using different timing to the left-hand, such that it does not fall conveniently in-line with the notes in the left-hand.

Example. 1

4/4 timing being equally divided by six.

Example. 2

Triplet timing that is in and out of sync with the left-hand.

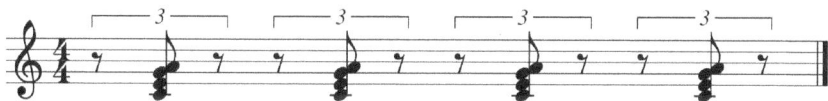

This kind of timing isn't the sort of thing that you would use for any long passages, it's better to use sparingly to create interest, so probably for one bar or two, or perhaps even just half a bar. It's a nice contrast to the general rhythmic feel of the piece, so it stands out well, grabs attention for a moment before falling back into the normal feel of the music.

Practice the next few examples to get the feel of the timing, if you've not come across this before then you might enjoy getting it right. It's not quite as difficult as it may first appear, as although the right-hand is at odds with the 4/4/ timing, it does fit in with the triplet feel of the left-hand. Once it clicks into place you won't have to think about it so much, which to a degree is a better way of approaching it, don't overthink it, just play. Definitely worth getting it down though, as it's good to throw this sort of thing into music from time to time while improvising.

Here the right-hand is split into six equal intervals. The 4/4 timing allows for twelve triplets in total (three per beat) so with a little mathematics, each chord will have the duration of two triplets. So although six notes doesn't divide nicely into the 4/4 timings four beats, it does match nicely with the left-hand because of the triplet timing. The right-hand is played on every other triplet.

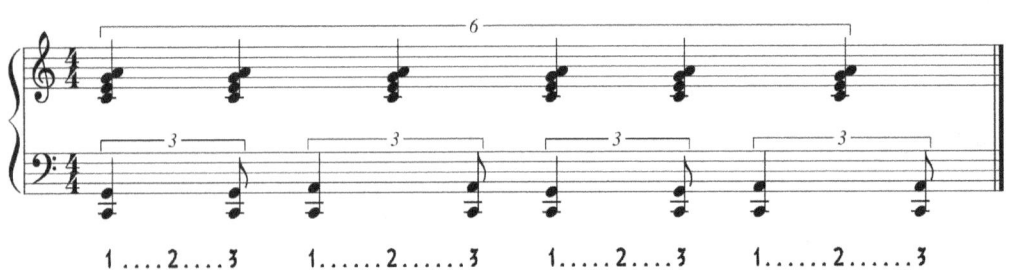

12-bar Practice Example. 1

27 AUDIO

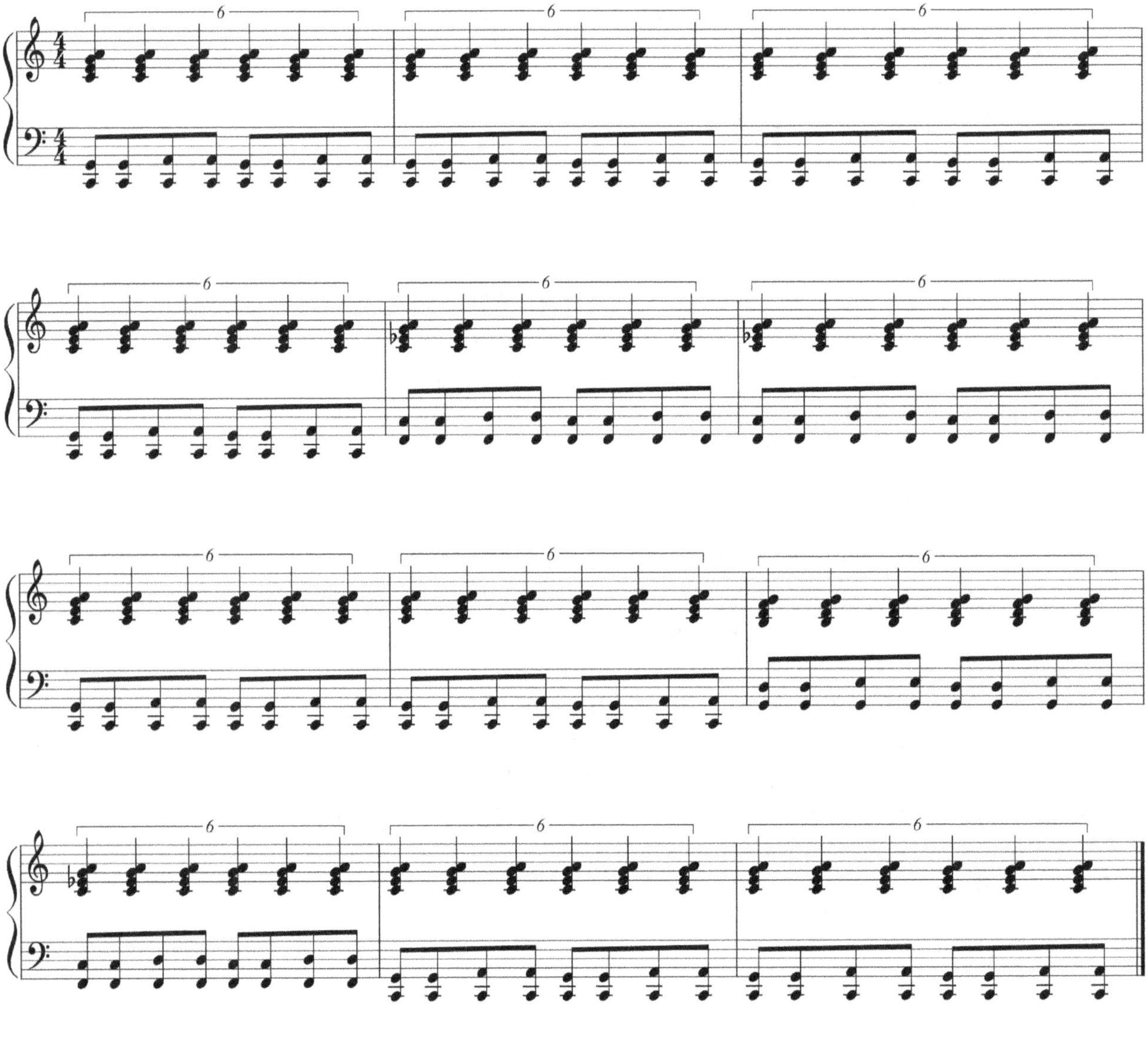

Here the right-hand chord is placed in the centre of each group of triplets. This is in contrast to the left-hand, as its notes are placed either side of the centre, so they never land in-line with each-other at any point.

12-bar Practice Example. 2

28 AUDIO

Next, the right-hand is played with a triplet rest between each chord. This results in some chords being in-line with notes in the left-hand, and some are not.

1.....2.....3 1.....2.....3 1.....2.....3 1.....2.....3

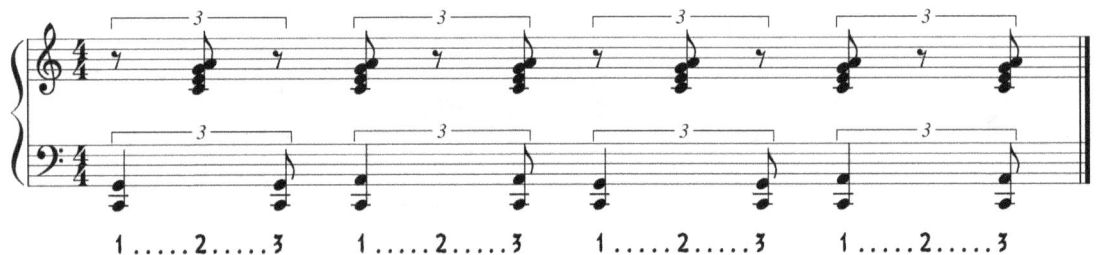

12-bar Practice Example. 3

29 AUDIO

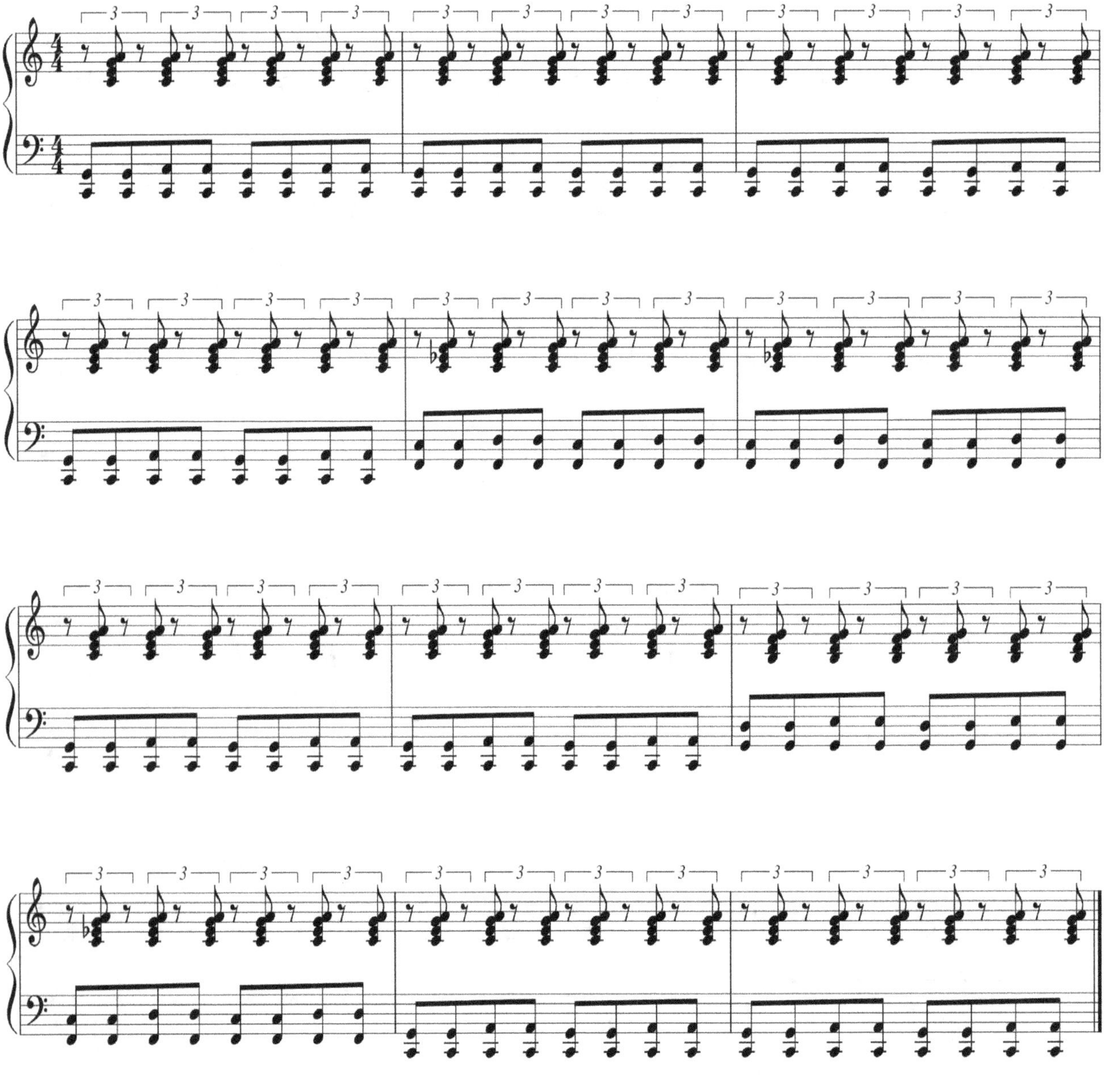

An Unusual Time

Rolling Chords

As I'm sure you know, an arpeggio is basically a broken chord whose notes are played in order, one after the other rather than instantaneously. This is found in every style imaginable, although instead of nice slow movements found in ballads and such like, here it tends to be done in quite a fast fashion. Sometimes it's in a repeated pattern that kind of rolls down the keys, because of this I'm referring to them as rolls or rolling chords. It's not an 'official' term, but it works for our purposes here with boogie-woogie quite well.

Typical ways of notating this are shown below, both equate to the same thing, it's just one has each note shown in order rather than implying.

Different Styles Of Notation

Example Of It Employed

A Rolling Chord

A full-on roll would look something like these. It's the same thing but repeated over an entire bar or two in a continuous rolling motion of sound. This is seen an awful lot in blues piano playing.

Or perhaps...

Rolling Chords 1

Use the twelve bar practice examples to get the feel of this under your fingers and then put them together in the short example boogie piece that follows them.

12-bar Practice Example

Rolling Chords 2

12-bar Practice Example

32 AUDIO

Boogie Rolling

33  AUDIO

Walking Bass-Lines

A walking bass is a bass-line that kind of walks up and down (in our case, up and down the keyboard rather than a fret board). This type of thing can be seen in various styles of music, which includes boogie-woogie piano.

Basic Used Notes

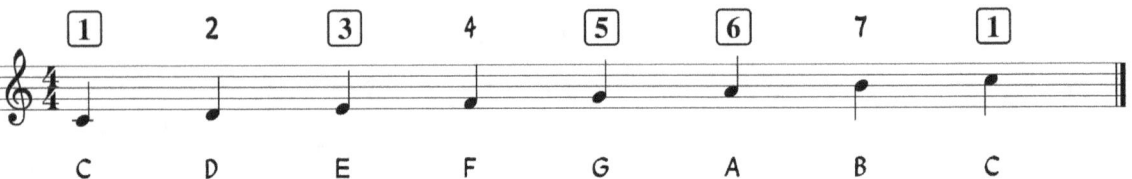

The starting point/basic notes for such a bass-line in boogie-woogie are shown above. The root, third, fifth, and sixth of the major scale are the basis of it, with the root often being used again at the top, an octave higher.

Typical Basic Pattern

A typical pattern is as follows, spread over two bars it moves up through the scale (one, three, five, six) and then back down through the scale (one, six, five, three).

> This is just the starting point of course, as the left-hand can potentially walk all over the place. In essence, any note can potentially work as long as it fits the context of the material it's based in, although some will obviously be used more often than others. This can be played as single notes, alternating octaves or even more chordal structures and is great fun to play around with.

Practice Example. 1

As the '**V**' and '**IV**' chords on bars nine and ten are only one bar long each, the pattern only walks up on each, not having the time/room to move back down again. If using two bars of the '**V**' chord instead then the pattern can be full length.

Practice Example. 2

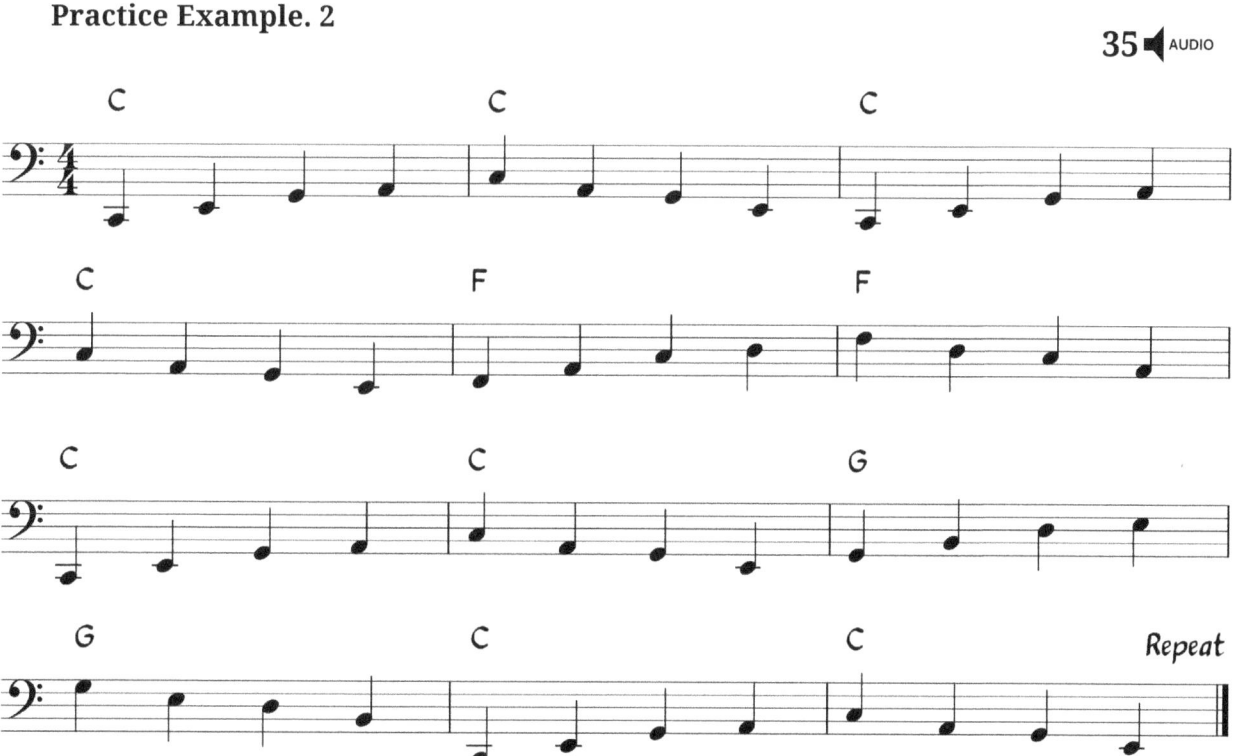

Walking Comp 1

This first example with both the walking left-hand and right-hand included keeps it simple to begin with, just a chord played every two beats over a single note left-hand. Practising some simple chords over the top is a good place to start to help with left/right-hand independence.

12-bar Example

Walking In Octaves

It's probably more common for boogie-woogie to use octaves in such patterns as it creates a bigger, more interesting sound compared to the single notes, which are perhaps more likely within a slow blues, or jazz piece, perhaps. The example uses the same notes as before, but played as octaves this time around.

Octaves Pattern

You will see this kind of thing in boogie-woogie music although sometimes only for small sections, as it's more common to see it in an alternating fashion (which we will look at soon). This is good practice in getting used to playing those octaves over the keyboard first though, as the notes will be the same.

12-bar Practice Example. 3

Walking Comping 2

This example uses octaves in the left-hand and now the chords are more frequent, playing on the off-beat creating a syncopated rhythm with the left-hand. Practising this pattern should help with left/right-hand independence and that constant syncopation is a great sound and very useful.

12-bar Example

36 AUDIO

Alternating Octaves

This is very typical of a walking boogie-woogie bass-line. Each note is played twice, alternating over an octave span.

Practising the octaves on the previous page may have helped somewhat. Although this is more difficult due to the extra movement, you have already been practising the positioning of the notes you will be using, it's just that now they are played alternately.

As always, get comfortable playing the left-hand individually before adding anything with the right-hand, as those two hands must be-able to work independently.

12-bar Practice Example. 4

Walking Comp 3

The first example with the alternating octave walking-bass goes back to having a chord played every two beats. Practising basic chords over the top is a good place to start while getting the left/right hands working together. Don't try to rush it, play at whatever tempo you can manage and only increase it gradually once you're happy.

12-bar Example

Alternative For 'V' And 'IV' Chords

When you only have one bar to play with (like on bars nine and ten), you can play the pattern as we have so far, or... Alternately on the last beat move back down to the third instead of moving up to the sixth, so it'll be **1-3-5-3** instead.

This helps a little with the '**V**' to '**IV**' chord change and to a lesser extent the '**IV**' to '**I**' change, as you are closer to the root note of the following chord.

12-bar Practice Example. 5

Walking Comp 4

Here we have the alternating octave left-hand played with the off-beat right-hand chords. Practising this rhythmic pattern should help with left/right-hand independence. If you have any, trouble just remember each chord is played at the same time as the second note (short part of the shuffle) of the left-hand (the top half of the octave). As a side point, note that both hands are an octave lower than previous examples.

12-bar Example

40 AUDIO

Walking Comp 5

The same left-hand pattern but here with a different right-hand rhythm that changes for the 'V' and 'IV' chords (which isn't an uncommon thing to do).

12-bar Example

41 AUDIO

Walking Comp 6

You could also use the shorter walking line (as used on the '**V**' and '**IV**' chords previously) for the entire piece, only moving up to the fifth on each bar.

12-bar Example

42 AUDIO

Addition Note (Flat-Seventh)

An additional note we can make good use of is the flat-seventh (as used in many other patterns).

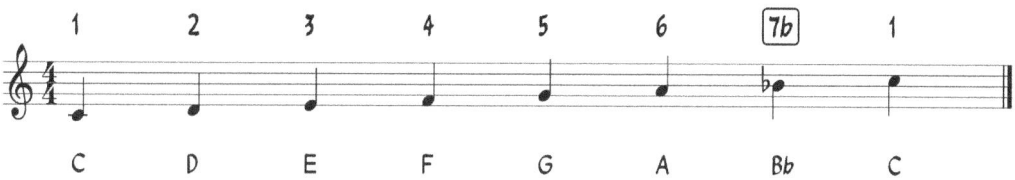

Pattern With Added Seventh

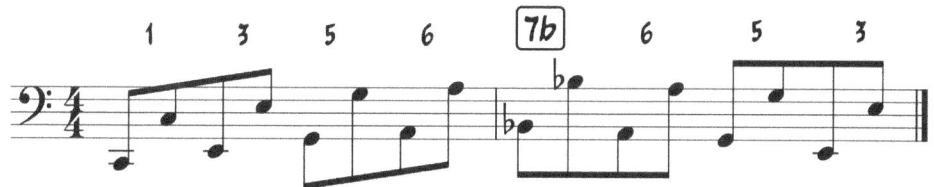

12-bar Practice Example. 6

43 AUDIO

Variations With A Flat-Seventh

1.

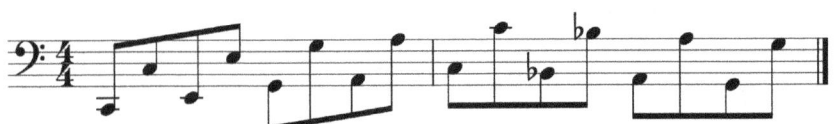

2.

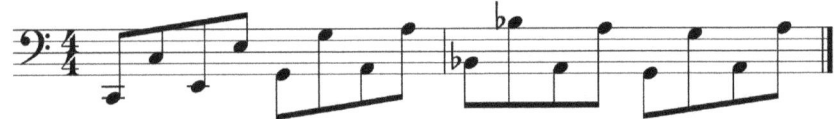

These variations are idea for using at the chord changes. Example one first for the '**I**' to '**IV**' change, example two for the '**I**' to '**V**' change. Both of these end two semi-tones within the root of the next chord.

12-bar Practice Example. 7

44 AUDIO

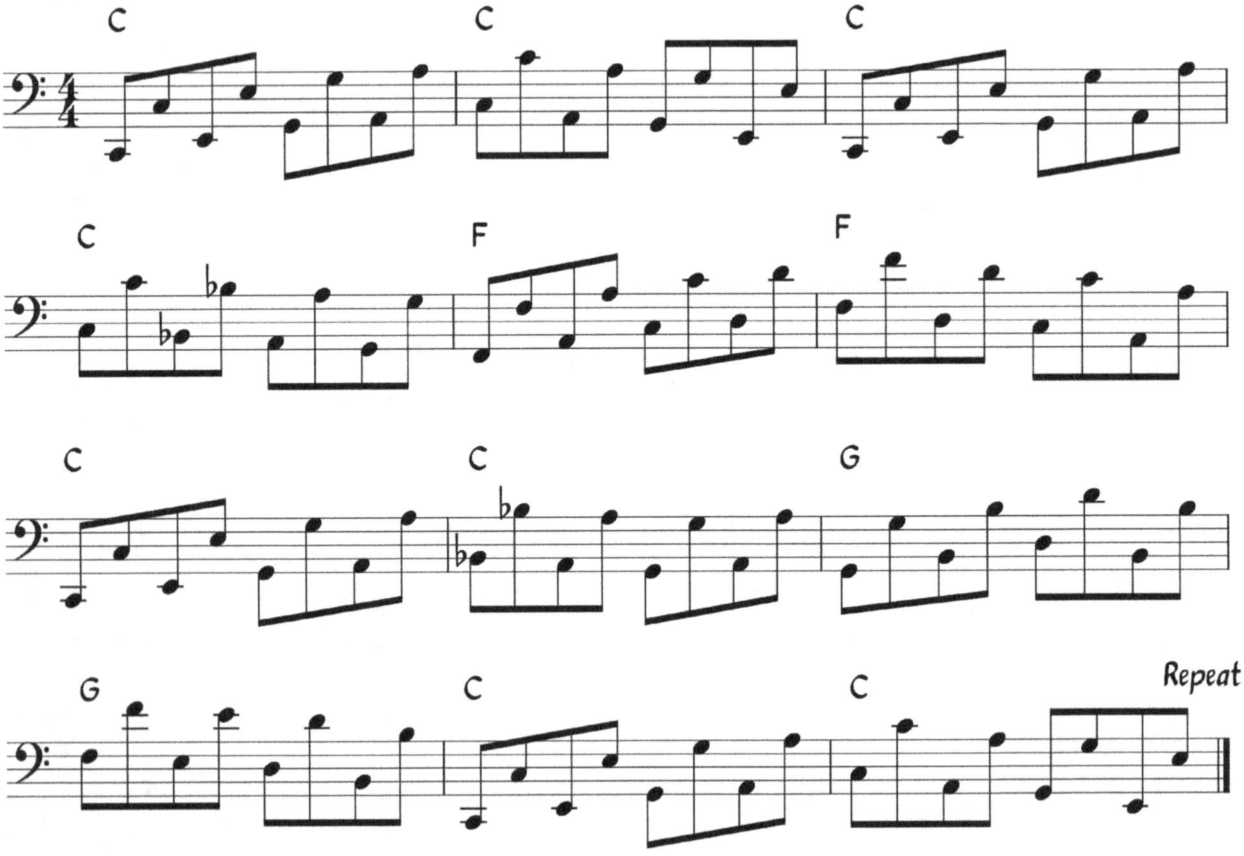

Walking Comp 7

This example uses a common (two chord per-bar) rhythmic pattern that should definitely be committed to memory. The left-hand uses the flat-seventh, but notice that it isn't used every single time. Mixing these things up stops it from becoming monotonous. Bars nine and ten are also both '**V**' chords this time around.

12-bar Example

Reverse Direction (Downwards Motion)

So far we have been walking the bass in an upward direction, but you can of course use the pattern in the opposite direction and walk down the keyboard.

Beginning the walk in a downwards motion tends not to be used as often, generally you tend to see the downward motion in small sections. For example, you might use an upward motion for the first four bars of '**C**' and then move downwards for the '**F**'. But it will be good practice to start with a downwards motion on all chords and although it's not as commonly used like this, it certainly works.

12-bar Practice Example. 8

Combining Up And Down Movements

Once you are comfortable with the walking-bass pattern in both directions, you can then begin to combine the two for an even more interesting left-hand. This makes it better to play and listen to, plus it allows you to flow from one chord to the next smoothly, and increase the range of the keyboard used.

Below we have the '**I**' chord moving upwards, but at the change to the '**IV**' chord we swap to a downwards motion. You will notice as you play that this is a nice, smooth transition, as the '**C**' chord ends one semi-tone (one-key) below the first note of the '**F**' chord.

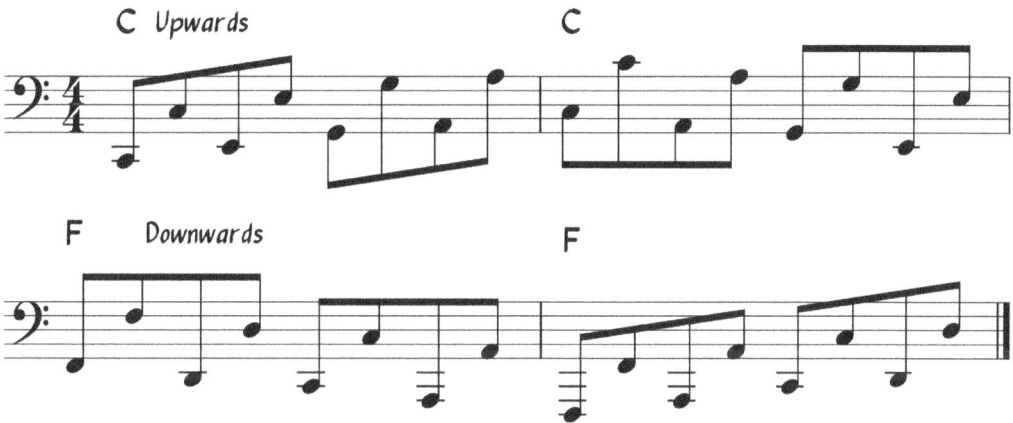

The next example shows the change from a '**V**' chord to a '**I**' chord. Moving downwards with the '**G**' we can finish one semi-tone below the first note (root) of the next chord again.

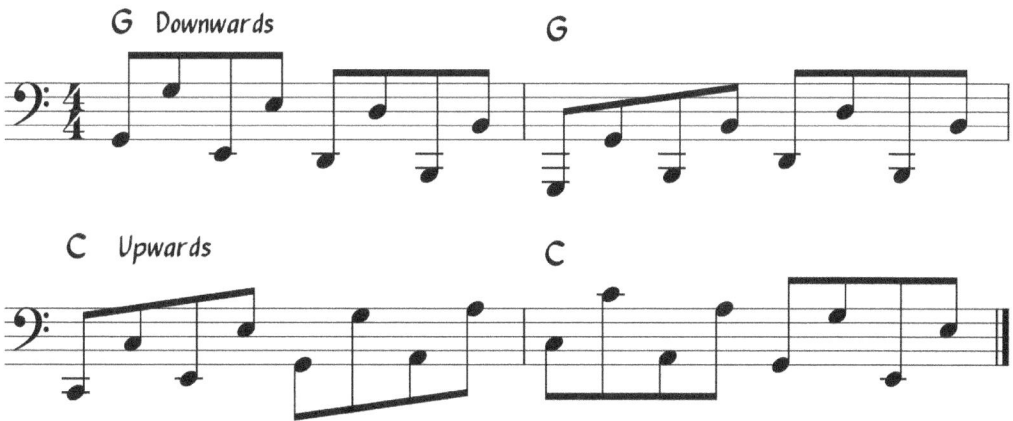

Up/Downwards Practice Example. 9

You can't always be one-semi-tone below the next root note at a chord change. The example below (found in the twelve bar above) has a three semi-tone step up, but it's still a small movement, which allows for smooth and consistent playing rather than large jumps across the keyboard, which can cause more problems.

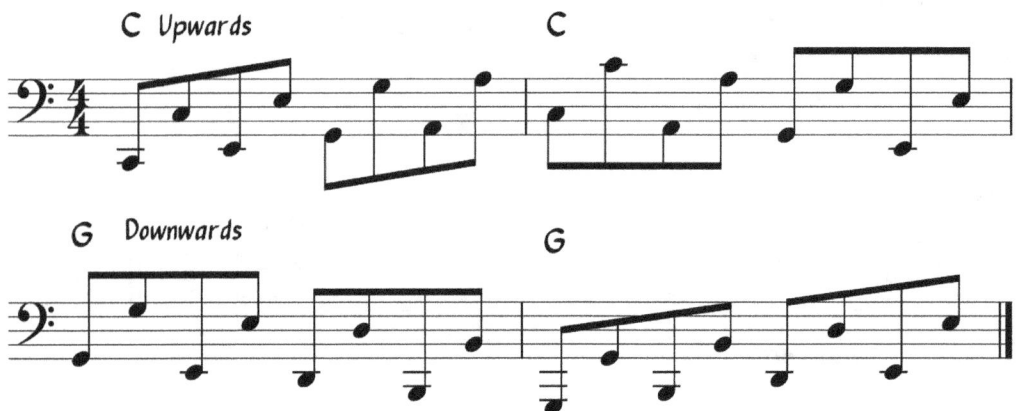

Walking Comp 8

This is another two chord per bar rhythmic pattern that should be committed to memory. Here the left-hand is both walking upwards and downwards at different points within the twelve-bars. While playing, you will see how much nicer it flows from one chord to the next.

12-bar Example

Walking Comp 9

A different rhythmic right-hand pattern, with the left-hand movements being varied again at different points.

Notice in bar-two how the left-hand and right-hand both use the same '**C**' key in beat-one, be careful when improvising that you don't get in a muddle with this kind of thing. In this example it works (just) as the notes don't quite coincide.

12-bar Example

49 AUDIO

Two-Octave Movements

While the tendency for the bass-line to walk up an octave and back down again is common place, there is nothing stopping you from moving over a longer range.

1.

Here the first four-bars of a twelve-bar progression sees you climb up two-octaves over the first two-bars and then back down over the second two.

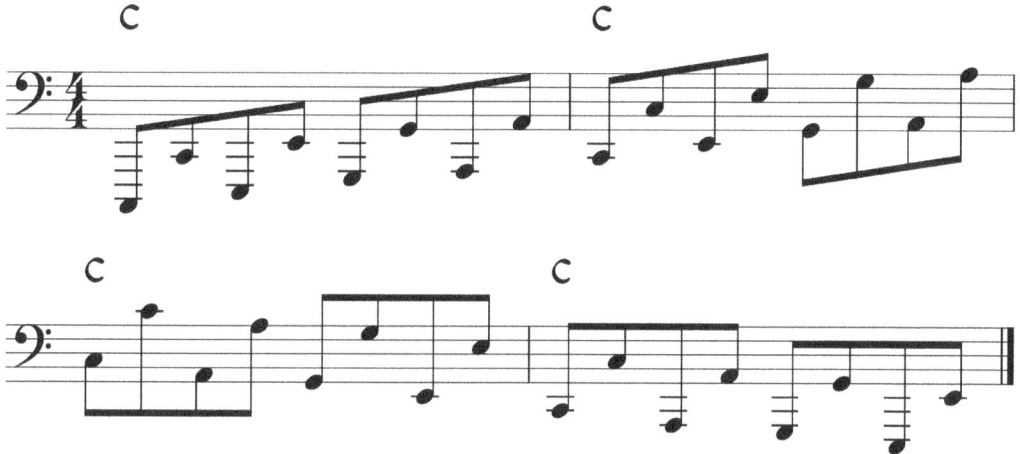

2.

Here bars nine and ten of a twelve-bar both use the '**V**' chord. This walks upwards for the two-bars and then at the '**I**' chord (bars eleven and twelve) it walks back down for two-bars.

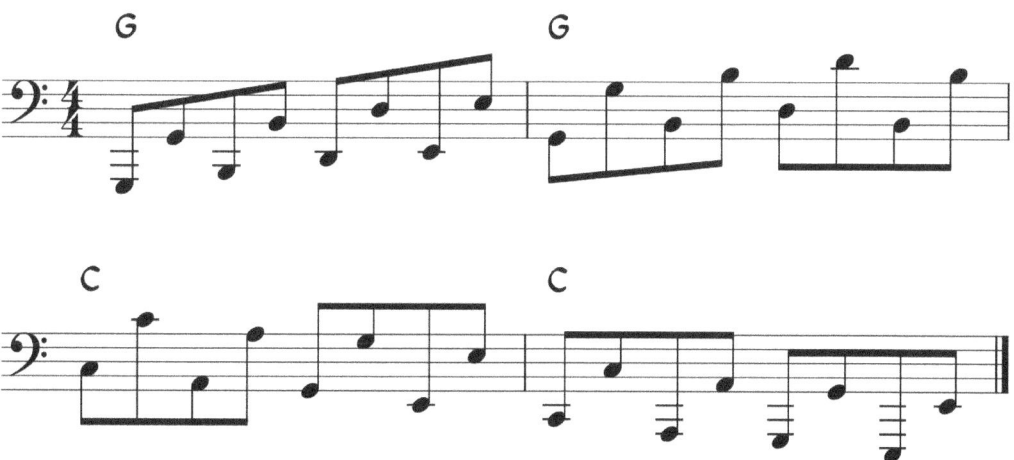

Have a practice with the two-octave walking movements over a full twelve-bar progression. Below is a quick breakdown of the different movements in this particular example.

Movement Breakdown

- Bar one sees the 'C' chord move up two-octaves, and then back down two-octaves.

- Bar five, changing to the 'F' chord, we find ourselves at the bottom of the keyboard with no room to move down again, so we walk upwards two-octaves.

- Bar seven changes to the 'C'. If we move upwards again, we will be interfering with the right-hand, so we move downwards.

- Bar nine changes to the 'G' chord. Being down low, the only space we have is to move upwards again.

- Bar eleven changes to 'C' chord. To move upwards would interfere with the right-hand, so we walk down for the last time.

12-bar Practice Example. 10

50 AUDIO

Another twelve-bar with different variation of upwards and downwards movements.

Movement Breakdown

- Bar one sees the '**C**' chord move up one-octave, then down two-octaves, and finally up one-octave.

- Bar five, changing to the '**F**' chord we find ourselves at the bottom of the keyboard, so we must walk upwards, this time only one-octave before moving back down.

- Bar seven changes to the '**C**' where we move upwards for one-octave, and then down for one.

- Bar nine changes to the '**G**' chord. Here we are mid-way on the keyboard, so we could move up or down, on this occasion we have gone down for two-octaves.

- Bar eleven changes to '**C**' chord, and we move up one-octave and then down one to finish.

12-bar Practice Example. 11

51 AUDIO

Additional 'IV' Chords

The twelve bar progressions we've been using for the walking left-hand have so far not included the **'IV'** chord on bars two and ten, so what are the options when including these two, how will they be played? Obviously you will only have one bar to play with, so there isn't time to move up and down again, so a shorter pattern is used. Below are a couple of examples for including it on bar-two (Being a **'I'** chord to **'IV'** chord and back to **'I'** chord movement).

'IV' Chord On Bar-Two

Here we have the 'IV' chord being used on bar-ten. Again it only gives you one-bar to play with, so the distance covered is minimal, below are a few ideas to consider trying.

'IV' Chord On Bar-Ten

1. Move up one octave on each chord using **1-3-5-3** on both chords.

2. Variation of above using **1-3-5-6** on both chords.

3. Move up on the '**V**' chord and down on the '**IV**' chord.

4. Continuous movement up through both the '**V**' and '**IV** 'chords.

Have a practice with these ideas over the following twelve-bar examples, and remember that these are only ideas, experiment and see where your hands take you.

12-bar Practice Example. 12

12-bar Practice Example. 13

Walking That Boogie

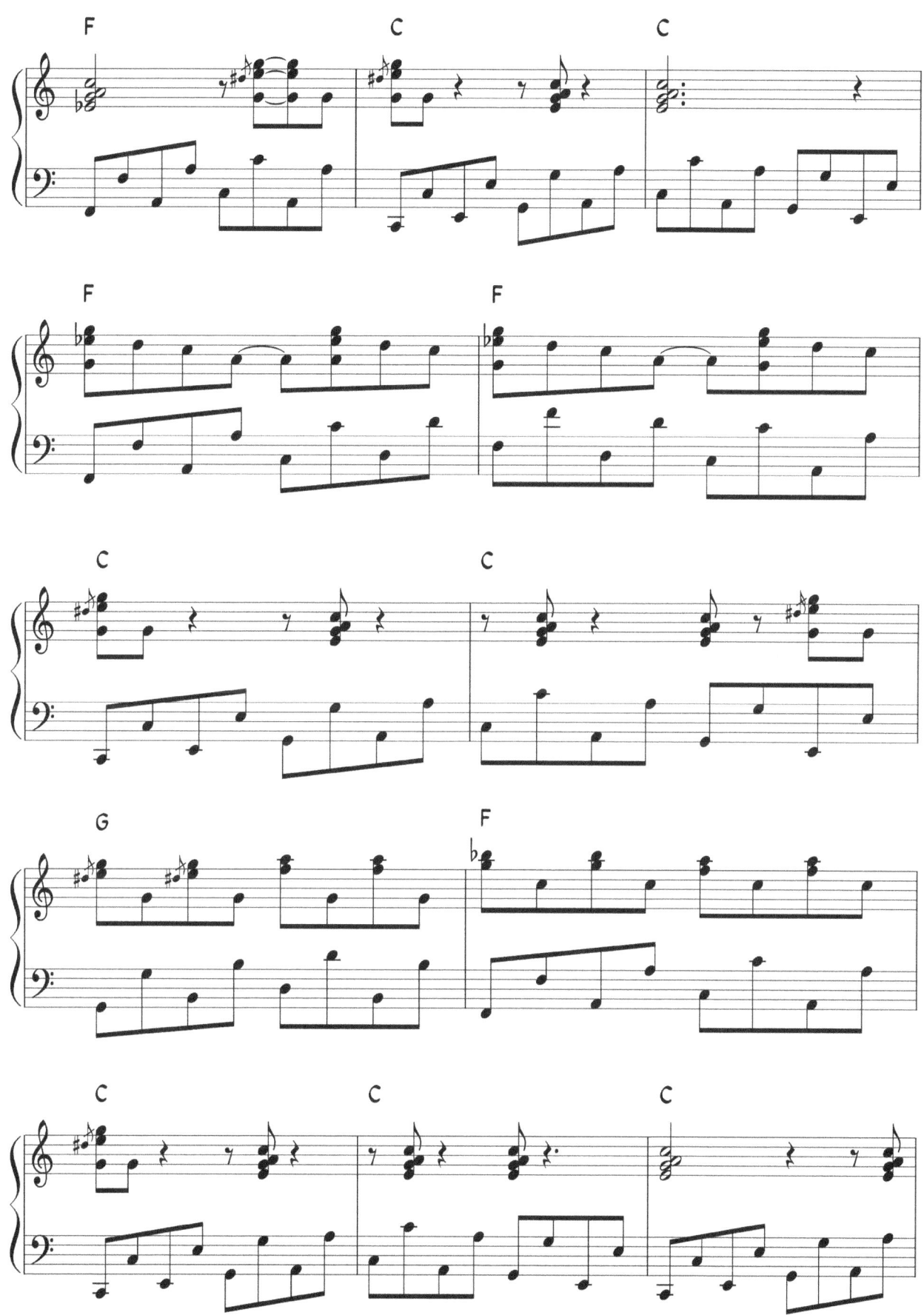

Chordal Variation. 1

As well as using single notes it is possible to play in a more chordal fashion, alternating between a single note and two notes, kind of like a broken chord.

One Note – Two Notes

This version has the single note at the bottom which then alternates with the two above.

Practice this over the twelve-bars below, but remember that all the options on the previous pages apply to this as well, it's essentially the same thing, it just has a little something added.

12-bar Practice Example. 14

Chordal Variation. 2

This version turns it around and has the two notes on the bottom and the single note played above. I prefer the sound of this one personally, plus it feels better on the hands, with a slightly less stressful movement. This is more like the left-hand that Ammons uses on the later sections of 'Stomp', although at times he may use a larger version, which we will also look at later.

Two Notes – One Note

Practice this over the twelve-bars below, but remember that all the options on the previous pages apply to this as well, it's essentially the same thing but with a little something added.

12-bar Practice Example. 15

56 AUDIO

Boogie Stomp 'V' Chord Difference

Just a side point regarding this pattern. The examples so far have followed it exactly through the chord changes, but transcriptions of Mr Ammons Stomp show him using the dominant-seventh within the 'V' chord rather than the major-seventh. It makes sense in the key of 'C' as it keeps it just on the white notes and the dissonance is either not noticed or adds flavour, depending on your perspective.

12-bar Practice Example. 16

Double Walking Boogie

Further Variations

If you wish, you can play this with an even fuller complement of notes by using a full triad on the bottom. Or taken further still, we could use four notes on the bottom chord and two on the top half. Bear in mind that this doesn't really suit a lot of keys due to the black keys making the movement very awkward, it works well in '**C**', although bear in mind that it's not overly easy.

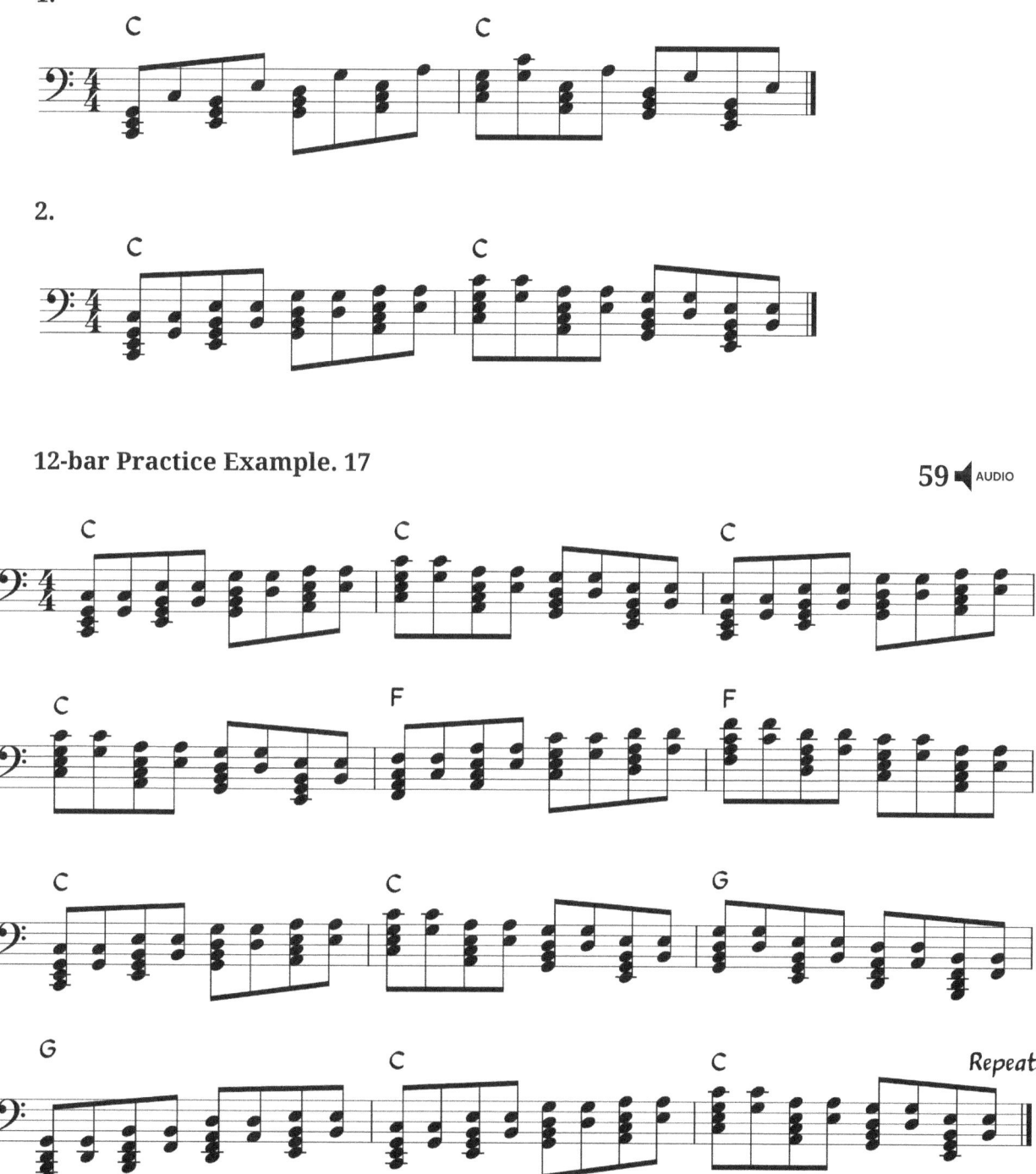

Further Walking

As stated earlier, although some notes are the foundation of the pattern (root, third, fifth) pretty much any note can be used if it works within the context of the piece. If it fits within the scale or the chords being used then it should be possible to incorporate it, especially as many of the notes can be considered passing notes.

It's also not always necessary to keep to a strict pattern as we have been doing so far, you can move around more using different patterns within the general up and down movement. How far you take this does depend somewhat on you're own tastes, as the more complex it becomes the further away from original boogie-woogie it becomes and further towards a jazz context. Not that that's a bad thing, it's down to taste.

Next we have three example twelve-bars that have the left-hand walking around in various different ways along with the standard patterns that we have already looked at.

12-bar Practice Example. 18

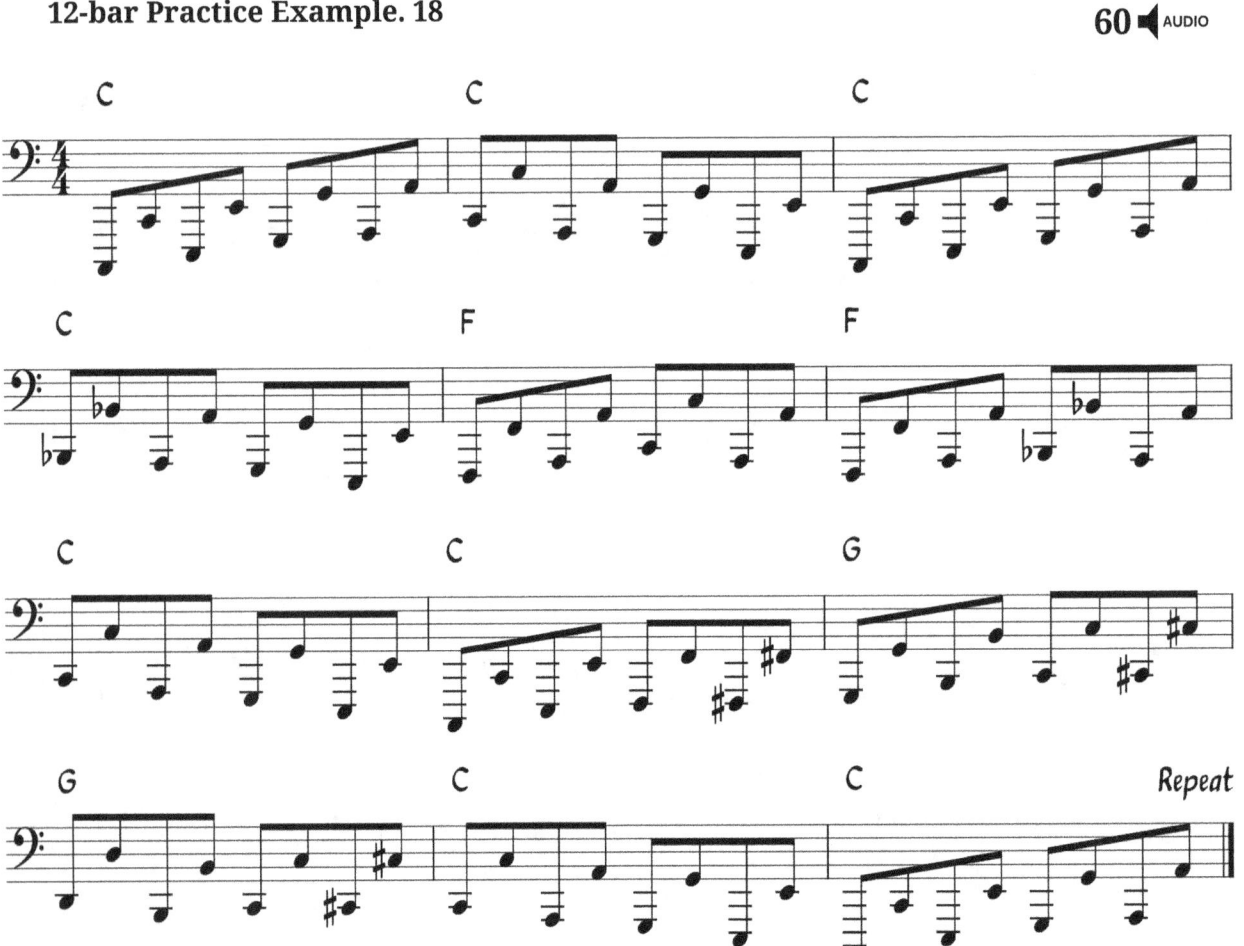

12-bar Practice Example. 19

12-bar Practice Example. 20

Differences Walking In Other Keys

Like most things with the piano, playing in the key of '**C**' is easier than most and this definitely goes for the walking style left-hand. In '**C**' the majority of notes used are white keys which allows for easy movement along the keyboard with your hand. The difficulty varies between keys, '**G**' or '**F**' aren't too bad as they both only use one flat between all three chords, so there's much obstruction to a smooth movement. If you look at a key like '**E♭**' instead, the left-hand on the '**I**' and '**IV**' chords (within a basic pattern) sees every-other key as a black one, which requires more hand movement.

Notes Used For 'C'

Keys in order of use. Smooth movement across the board.

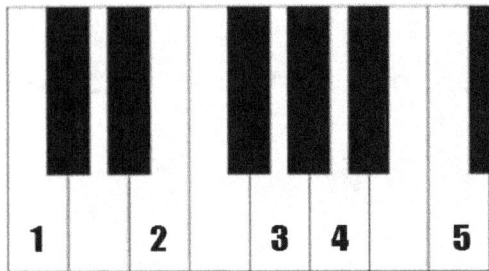

Notes Used For 'E-flat'

Keys in order of use. Extra motion in and out of the keyboard.

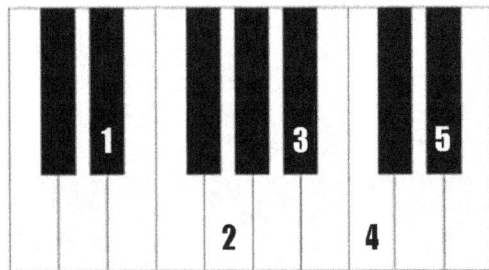

Next are a couple of example pieces to have a play with in the keys of '**F**' and '**E♭**'. It's not practical to have examples of everything in all keys in a book, so remember to play around, practice and improvise in as many keys as you can, you will thank yourself in the long-run.

Walking Keys Boogie

Flat Foot Boogie

64  AUDIO

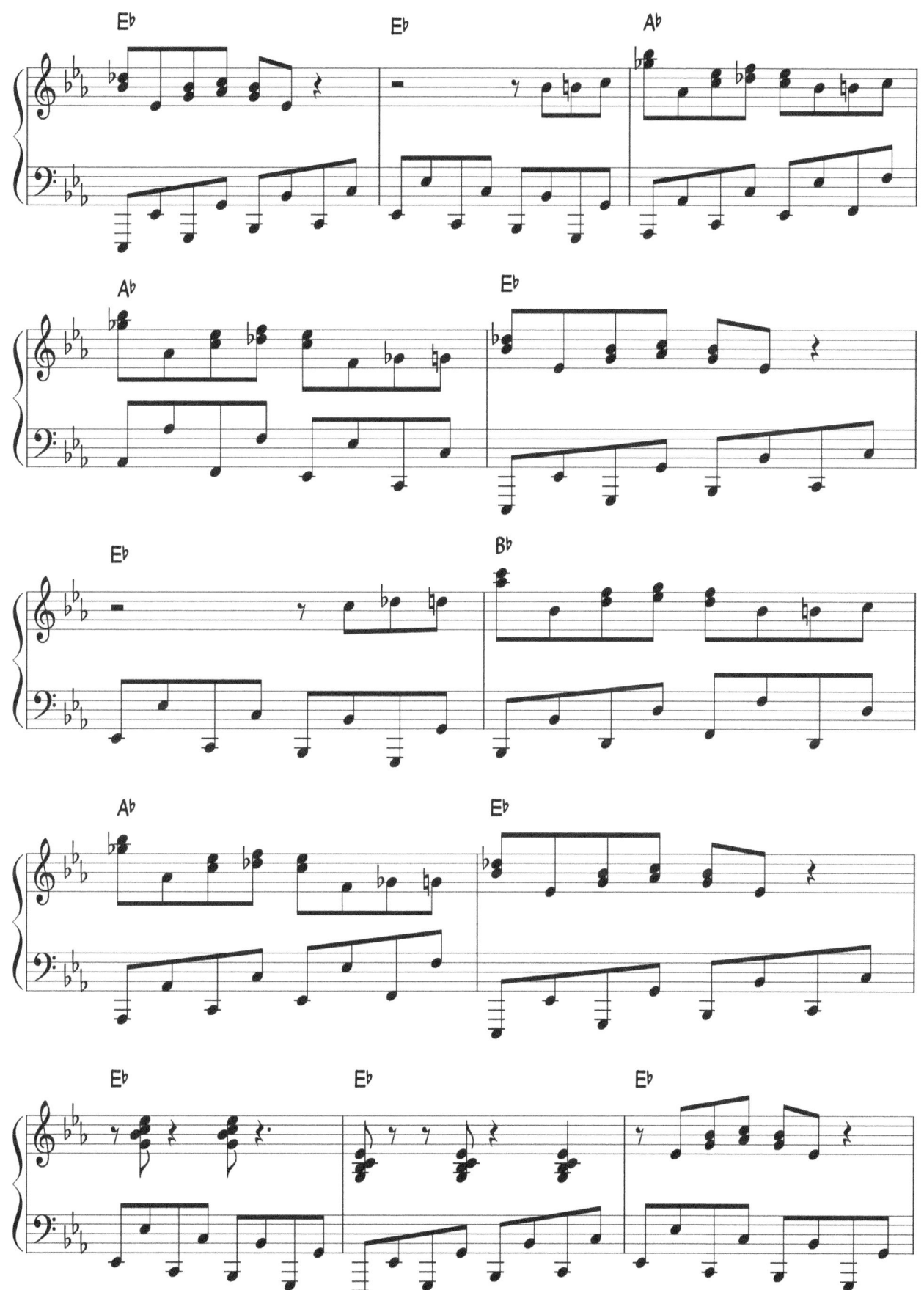

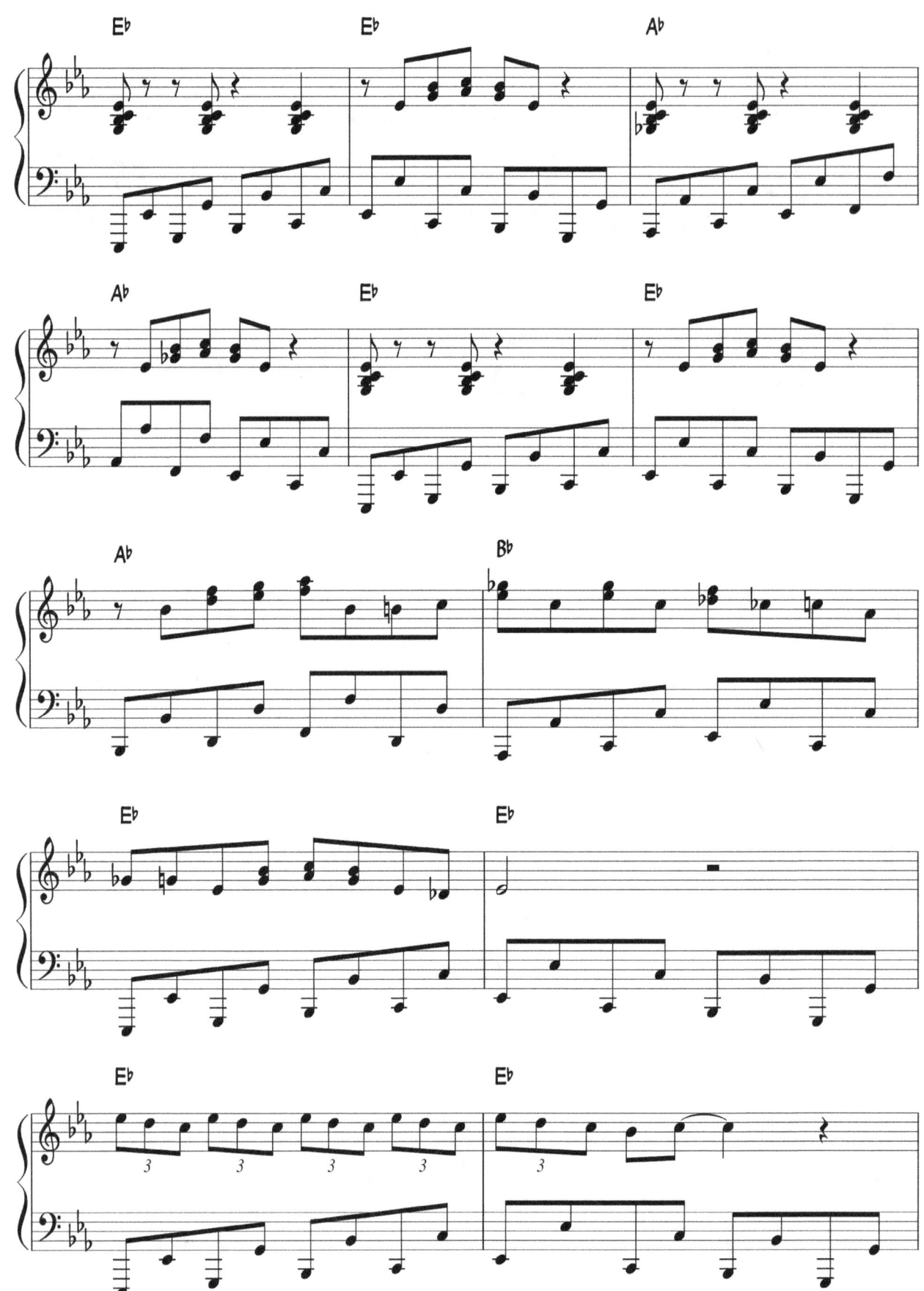

Left-Hand Pattern 4

This style left-hand pattern can also be heard in rock 'n' roll, variants of which have appeared in some classic songs. There are different ways to play what is essentially the same riff which consists of the root, third, fifth and sixth, moving up from the root to the top with a slight alternating movement.

12-bar Practice Example

65 AUDIO

Being constructed entirely from single notes (one note being played at any one time) it is possible to play this at quite a high tempo, perhaps up to 180bpm for example. Some variants (which we'll look at afterwards) double up on notes at different points, making it a little more challenging to play at higher tempos.

Comping 10

Once you can play the left-hand effectively move on and practice it with a simple right-hand to get used to playing with both hands. Every left-hand pattern takes time to assimilate properly, as they really need to be independent.

12-bar Practice Example

Waterfall Boogie

Pattern Variations

These variations of the left-hand extend over into two bars instead of one, with the exception of bars nine and ten that remain unchanged. These can all be mixed together if you wish to use them as such.

Chord Run Up

In the example piece just gone (on page.116) there is a kind of run up of chords over the 'V' and 'IV' chords. This uses the triads made up from the major scale from the key it is in, in this case that's the key of 'C'.

Triads Of 'C' Major Scale

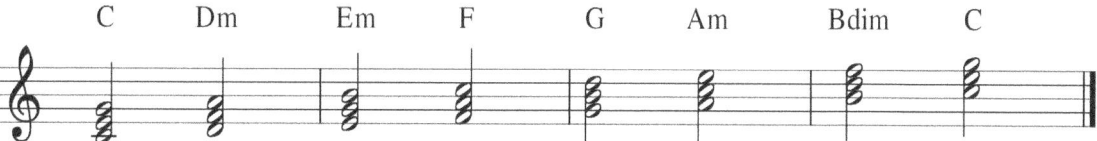

In the previous example piece the run began on the 'G' chord and moved through the scale twice before ending on another 'G' two-octaves higher up. This looks and sounds quite impressive, although in theory the idea is quite simple.

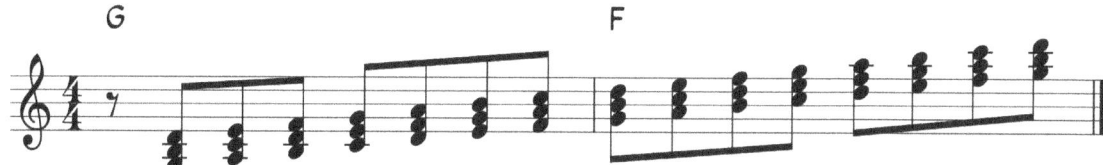

Use In Other Keys

That example was in the key of 'C' which meant that all the notes used for the triads were white keys. This made the movement relatively easy compared to the same idea in other keys which incorporate black keys. Try the same run again but transposed to A-flat.

In The Key Of 'A♭'

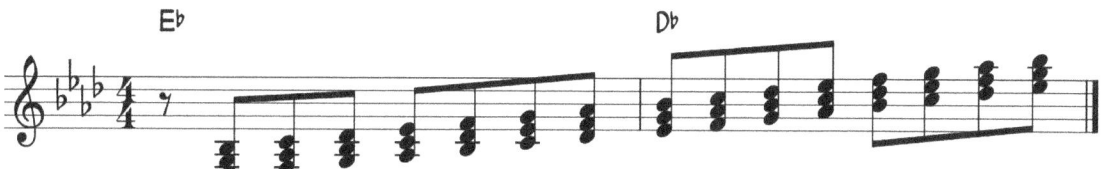

> Having four-flats makes this far more challenging, so it's probably best left as a trick in 'C'. That said, feel free to play around with it and if it falls under your fingers without too many issues in other keys, then certainly use it.

Left-Hand Pattern 5

This pattern is very similar to the previous one as you may well notice, but at the same time it is quite different to play. The root note is now played on every measure, doubling up with the third, fifth, and sixth in an alternating fashion. This makes it a little harder to play in a physical sense. Optionally this works well at a slower pace as well as a fast tempo. So anything 120-180 bpm, perhaps. The tempo does change the feel of the pattern a fair degree.

12-bar Practice Example

If played at a slower tempo, I like to accent the first notes of beats two and four a little, it adds more feel to the pattern, although it's completely optional.

Comping 11

Have a practice of this left-hand using a simple right-hand until you get the feel of it. It's intended to be played approximately around 120 bpm, so a relatively relaxed pace compared to some boogie. This combined with the accents on the off beats (two and four) create a great sound, in my opinion anyway, you can decide for yourselves. Once you're happy with playing it, move on to the example piece on the next page.

12-bar Practice Example

71 AUDIO

Boogie Jump

In Other Keys

You might well be playing in all manner of different keys already, but in case you aren't doing so, coming next is the first twelve-bar section of the last piece, shown in several keys that are commonly used.

This will give a little taste of how some keys feel different to play than others, due to the differing keys used creating different shapes over the key-bed. The more black keys that are used the more complicated the movement over them tends to become, with **'B'** being trickier than **'C'** for example. Some keys will seem more comfortable for sure, while some will be similar to each-other to some degree.

Each key also has its own sound, and although we are talking about playing the same piece, changing the key can alter the way the music sounds. Some things sound better in some keys than others, but then you could say this is down to taste. For me, out of the keys I've included **'A'** doesn't work for me so well for this particular piece (sound wise). Also, the pattern it creates over the key-bed is less than inviting, try it and decide for yourself.

Another difference is the direction of movement at the chord changes. It's pretty common practice to move upwards **(see example. B)** when you change from the **'I'** chord to the **'IV'** chord for instance. But in some keys this can mean the left-hand on the **'IV'** and **'V'** chords may seem a little high up on the key-bed, so you have the option to move the left-hand down at the change instead **(see example. C)**. This does two things, for one it keeps the bass lower which for the majority of the time is preferably (it is the bass, although at times it's good to move upwards for a time.) Secondly, it frees up space on the key-bed for the right-hand to move down lower which gives you more options of where to play.

Left-hand Movement Options

Key Of 'G'

Key Of 'A'

Left-Hand Tenths

There are some left-hand patterns that might not look especially hard on paper, but can be a real challenge or even sometimes even impossible to play. The sort of thing I'm talking about uses tenths.

Example Of Tenth Interval

As the scale above quickly highlights, a tenth is quite a stretch, because of this some people will find it extremely difficult or even impossible, when others can manage it okay, it depends on the size of your hands and there's not much we can do to change that. Some players have great big paws and can use tenths with no problem.

Personally, I can only make the stretch over certain chords. '**C**' or '**G**' for example are possible, '**D**' is pushing it and '**E**' is just about impossible. It's frustrating, as tenths create a really nice sound, but you can't win them all.

There are two ways around this problem (not just in boogie-woogie, but piano playing in general).

1. **Don't use tenths**

Admittedly this doesn't improve your playing, but it certainly does solve the problem.

2. **Jump/Roll Your Hand**

Play the root and the tenth separately. The root is first, followed by the tenth (and anything you wish in-between them) but you hold the notes with the sustain pedal (and so blend them together). In a faster boogie-woogie setting, too much pedal can make a muddy sounding mess, so it's still a nice challenge.

Left-Hand Pattern 6

This pattern uses tenths throughout and may create quite a challenge for you depending on your hand span. Also, due to its nature you won't be playing this at lightning speed, around 120 bpm is probably about as fast as you'd want/need.

The positioning of the keys also means that it won't work too well in all keys, although that is up to yourselves to decide if it is practical for you.

12-bar Practice Example

77 🔊 AUDIO

Although the root and tenth aren't ever played at the same time, it is still a considerable stretch due to the consistent nature of the root and tenth. You can kinda roll your hand from one side to the other to a degree, but you can't really move your hand too far out of position, as ideally it needs to hover over the notes. This is different to playing a slow ballad (for example) where you can hold the root with the pedal as you move over to the tenth.

Alternative Option (Octaves)

If playing the tenths is really not an option for you (and that's probably a reasonable number of people) then an alternative version of the pattern is to swap out the tenths for octaves.

As you can probably tell, this doesn't sound quite as good. It's lacking the harmonic interest of the tenths in the original, but it's certainly a lot more useable for the majority of us that can't realistically stretch to the tenths in this manner.

12-bar Practice Example

78 AUDIO

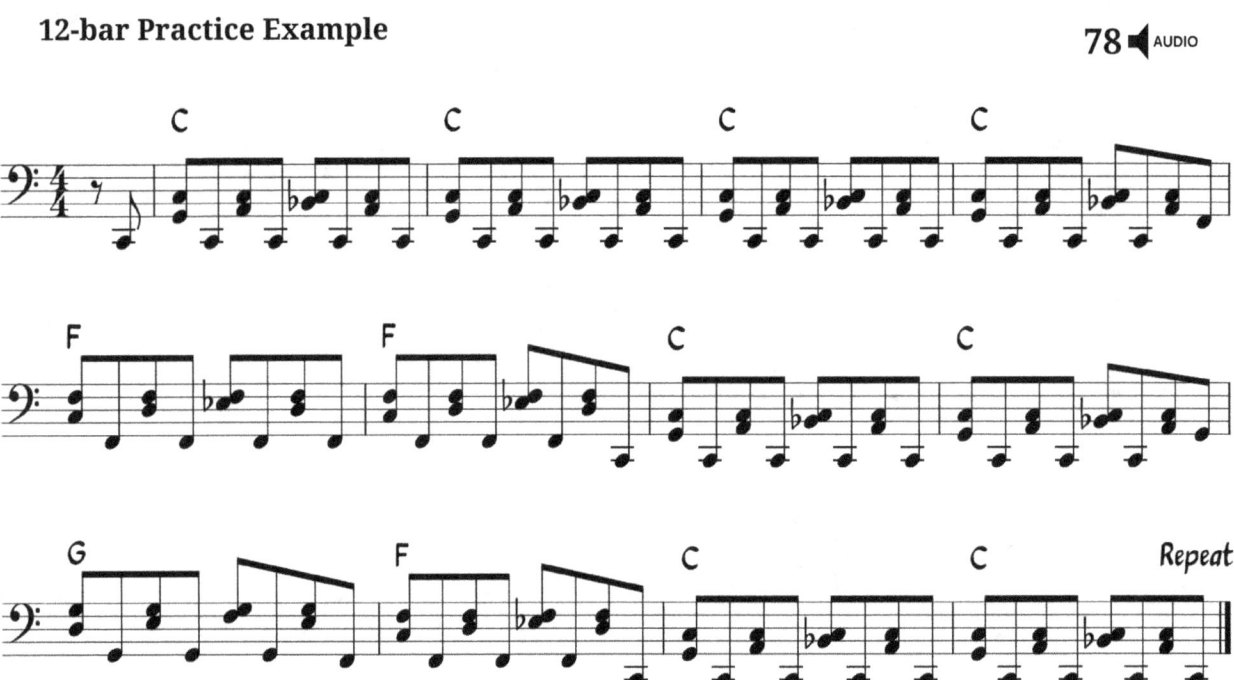

> Both versions of this use the root note of the preceding bar as the last note of the previous bar at the chord changes. This pre-emptive technique makes the jump to the next chord as smooth as possible. This was also covered in volume-one, as it's a common technique used on a lot of left-hand patterns.

Pattern With Octaves

This version uses octaves with the left-hand rather than the tenths. It lacks the harmonic interest of the tenths, but the trade-off is that it's more practical to play unless your hands are suitable sized for the longer stretch.

12-bar Practice Example

Pattern With Tenths

Here you have the full version with the tenths. It does arguably sound better, but not everyone can stretch to play it. Personally I can just reach enough to play in this key, although it's really not very comfortable. If you struggle, try to roll your hand from one side to the other, rather than keeping all fingers hovering over all the keys, it might work for you, it might not.

12-bar Practice Example

Playing Other Keys

While the octave version should work to some extent in most keys (some better than others) the tenth version doesn't necessarily, or at least not without some changes in places.

Fingering For Pattern In 'C'

You can see the fingering used in the pattern for a 'C' chord. The little finger can stay at the bottom, the thumb at the top, leaving the second finger to move freely between the other notes unencumbered. It's certainly a stretch, but it works.

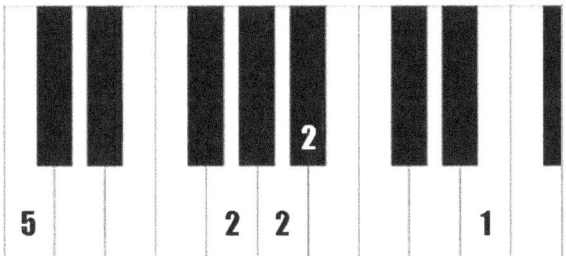

What About A Different Key?

If for example you were to play this in the key of '**G**' you would use the chords **G - C - D**. As we saw above, the '**C**' chord works fine and so will the '**G**', but this pattern over the '**D**' chord will cause some issues.

Fingering For Pattern In 'D'

Here you have two issues to contend with. One is that the distance required between the thumb and little finger is greater, making an already long stretch... longer. Secondly is that the second finger can't move so freely. Having the thumb by the **F-sharp** forces the hand towards the fall-board, resulting in the **B-flat** obstructing the **A-key** to **B/C-keys** movement.

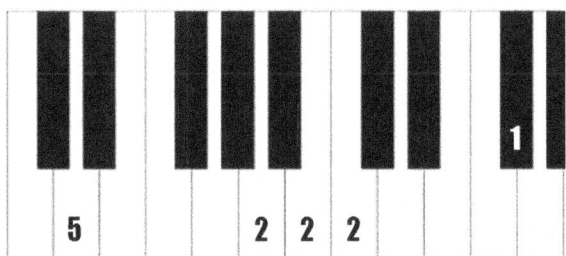

You can see in the photos how the second finger is stuck behind the **B-flat**, making it necessary to actually lift the finger over the key in order to reach the **B-key** that follows.

Second On 'A'   **Second On 'B♭'**

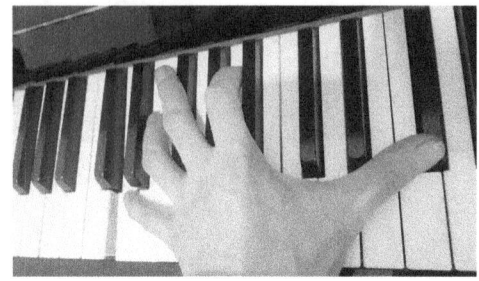

Try it for yourself, but it is an extremely awkward position. Because of this I wouldn't recommend using the pattern in the key of **'D'** like above for instance. Only use something where it really works rather than waste time with the impossible.

In the key of **'G'** that we mentioned earlier, only the **'V'** chord causes issues (being the **'D'** yet again) so it's best to change it to something else for that particular bar rather than struggle.

Alternatives

1.

2.

3.

4.

Tenths Boogie

Here we have the same music as before but transposed into the key of **'G'**. This actually required a few changes to the music, as the **'I'** chord left-hand needed to move up an octave to sound less muddy, which in turn required the right-hand to move up out of the way. The left-hand on the **'IV'** and **'V'** chords has also changed to an alternative due to the pattern not being ideal for the **'D'** chord.

12-bar Practice Example

Tenths Boogie Alternate

Here with have some alternate options for the left-hand. The basic pattern is the same, but we now have a walk-down on bar-four to the chord change. The left-hand on the 'V' chord is a variation and bar-ten has a walk-up using tenths.

12-bar Practice Example

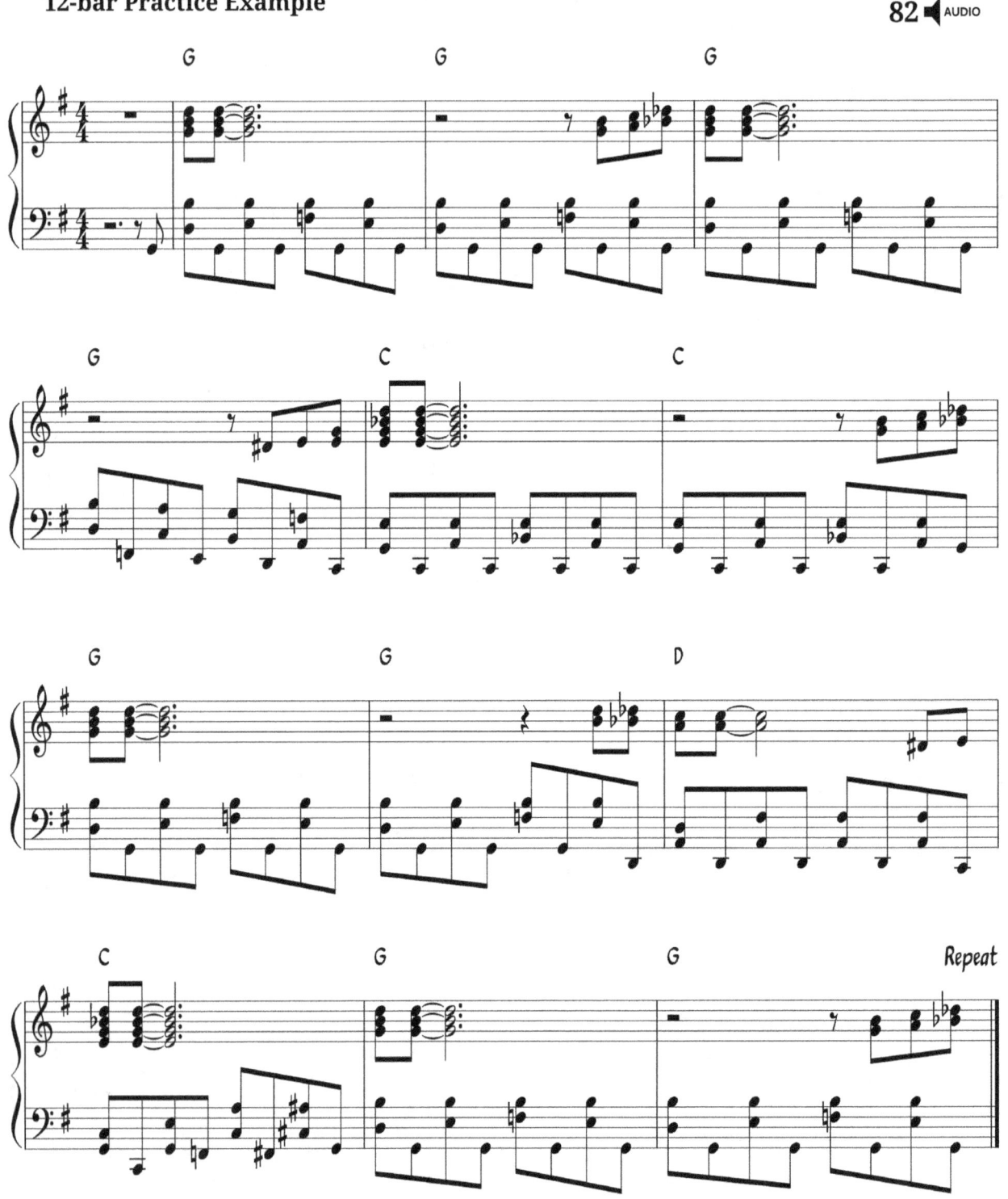

Adding Some Stride

Stride piano is a style of playing that is based around having a bass note followed by a chord in an alternate fashion, moving up and down the keyboard with the left-hand. Now while this isn't generally a boogie-woogie thing, it can be used in places to good effect, one of these times is on the '**V**' chord and also sometimes the following '**IV**' chord. This works well as it breaks up the repetitive patterns and so sounds interesting.

Basic Example

You can see how it moves from the root note up to a chord and then down to the fifth before return back up to the chord. It can be done in various ways, but this is the basic idea.

Chord Variations

1.

Larger chord with root repeated at the top.

2.

Seventh chord without the fifth.

3.

Seventh chord without the third.

A discussed before, boogie-woogie isn't a stride style as such, so this is only being used on bars nine and ten with the '**V**' and '**IV**' chords. Have a practice of this over a twelve bar progression without any right-hand to begin with, switching from the tenths pattern to the stride part and then back again.

12-bar Practice Example

As always, you're looking to acquire independence between the two hands. With the left-hand doing its own thing while you play over the top with the right-hand, so it's vital to get it down to some degree before considering adding anything with the right-hand.

> You may notice how the simple crochets feel a little out of place perhaps, lacking the feel of the rest of the music, and I would agree. So, we need to add a little something to this to make it a bit more musical.

Adding A Shuffle Feel

Each chord is now shorter (two triplets duration) as the beat is now split in order to add the additional note.

84 AUDIO

Alternative. 1

The root note is now also split within the beat, with the chord itself being split, with the root being played before the rest of it. This note can be tied to the chord if you prefer.

85 AUDIO

Alternative. 2 (Tied)

86 AUDIO

Alternative. 3

Alternatives three, four, and five use different combinations of the same octave-bass and chord patterns.

87 AUDIO

Alternative. 4

88 AUDIO

Alternative. 5

Alternative. 6

This has added extra movement in the way of a short walk-up at the end of bar-one. This movement could also be used when moving to another chord, like 'I' to 'IV'.

Alternative. 7

A variation of the walk-up on the first bar, adding a little extra to it that just stretches into the next bar.

Alternative. 8 (With Chord Change 'V' to 'IV')

The walk-up pattern is used to move into the chord change

Alternative. 9

Here the pattern moves through two chord changes. 'V' to 'IV' at the end of bar-one, and 'IV' to 'I' at the end of bar-two.

Example 12-Bar. 1

Example 12-Bar. 2

Example 12-Bar. 3

96 AUDIO

Example 12-Bar. 4

97 AUDIO

Additional Stride On Bars Five And Six

So far we've used the stride patterns within bars nine and ten, but you don't have to limit it to these only. The standard pattern over the '**IV**' chord on bars five and six can also be substituted for a stride style replacement.

Bars Used With Stride Patterns

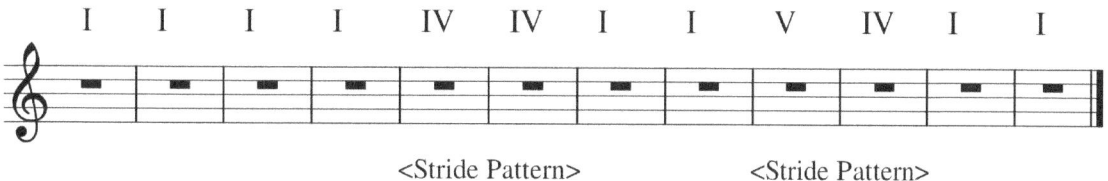

Example 12-Bar. 5   (Additional Substitution)

98 AUDIO

The song example on the following pages takes the different patterns we have looked at and uses a different one in each twelve bar section, along with the right-hand becoming gradually busier as it moves along.

Stride Along Boogie

293

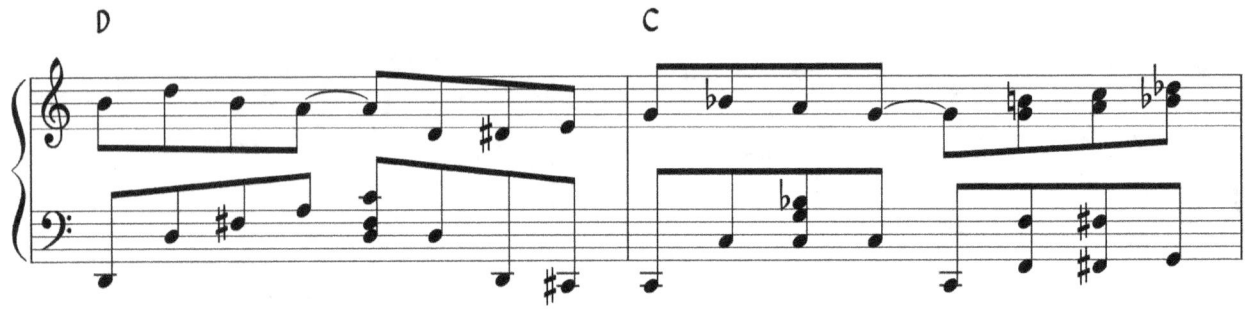

IMPROVISING
BOOGIE-WOOGIE

Volume Three

Left-Hand Pattern 1

Before we get started on the improvisation side of things, let's get warmed up with this great little left-hand pattern. Based around the root, third, fifth and sixth, it's unusual in that it also includes the fourth as a stepping stone up to the fifth.

12-bar Practice Example

A couple of variations are shown below, the differences are minor, so play whichever version you prefer. Personally I use either the top one or variation two.

Variation. 1

Variation. 2

Boogie On Fourth

302

Using Thirds

It's quite common to hear riffs and even whole passages created using thirds. Often they are mixed with other ideas, but at times they can be used solely on their own, creating a riff or a run down the keyboard using nothing but thirds. Learning them all, having them memorised and practised sufficiently to recall when playing without thought is really useful for improvising.

Third Interval

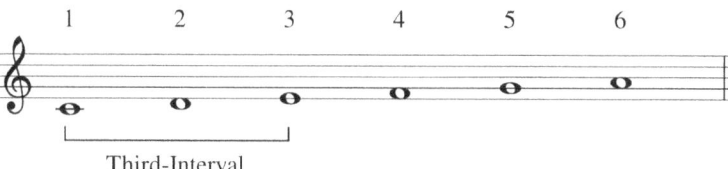

As shown in the diagram above, a third is two notes that are three intervals apart. The second note is two steps (through the scale) higher than the first. This applies to all positions throughout the scale.

Third Interval Examples

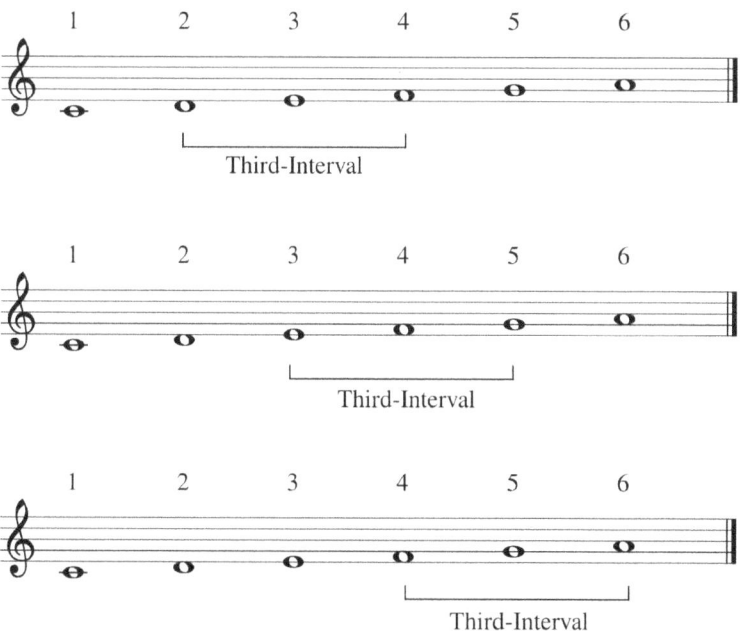

Let's start by looking at the thirds created from the major scale. I will point out straight away that this is very limiting and not entirely suited for our purpose (although usable at times) so afterwards we will move on to add some more interesting options to it.

Thirds Built On 'C' Major

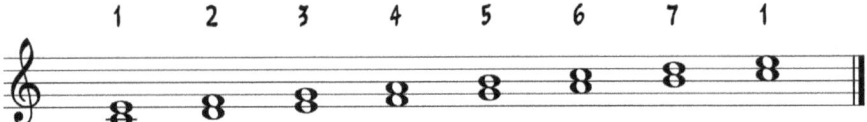

Here we have the thirds built from the major scale, each one is built upon the intervals of the scale. They're easy to remember as essentially it's just the major scale, but with an extra note added above. You can see three more examples of this built upon the '**F**', '**G**' and '**D**' major scales below.

Thirds Built In Key Of 'F'

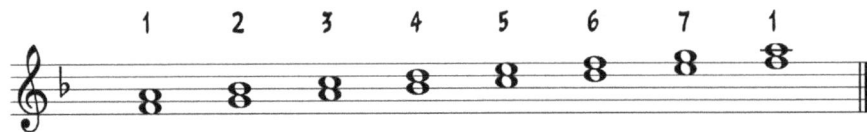

Thirds Built In Key Of 'G'

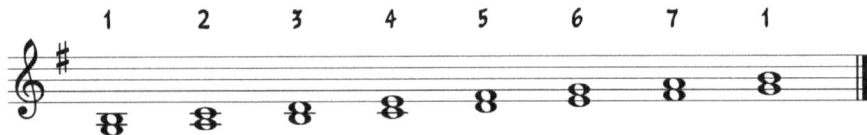

Thirds Built In Key Of 'D'

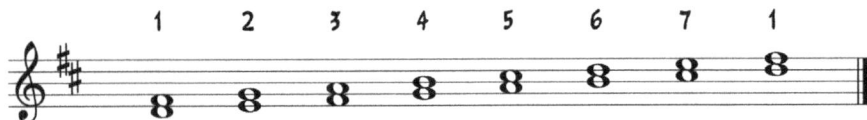

If you know your major scales then it's easy to work out the thirds for whatever key you are in, even if it's a key you haven't really been working with.

So with the basics over, let's put them into context and see how they work within boogie-woogie. You'll see how the ones used here fit perfectly, but you may notice two things. It lacks that blues sound, it's too upright and... well, major. Also, that we have stayed away from certain thirds, two in particular as they contain the major-seventh which clashes somewhat, so this needs altering for them to be more useable.

Example 12-bar (Using Only Major Thirds)

Additional Thirds

So having looked at the basic thirds built upon the major scale, we have seen that being entirely from the major scale they lacked something of the blues element that we require here. Step in the flat/dominant seventh.

Thirds With Flat-Seventh (Key Of 'C')

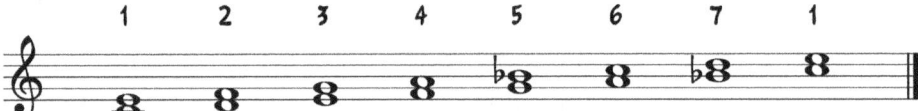

For the most part we have the same scale, except we are replacing the major-seventh with the flat/dominant seventh. This note is from the minor pentatonic, minor blues scale and Mixolydian mode. All of these are more suitable for boogie-woogie duty than the good old major scale.

Thirds With Flat-Seventh (Key Of 'F')

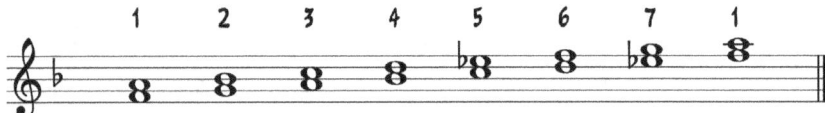

Thirds With Flat-Seventh (Key Of 'G')

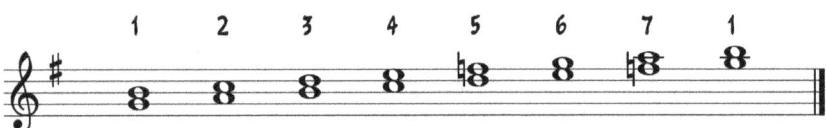

Thirds With Flat-Seventh (Key Of 'D')

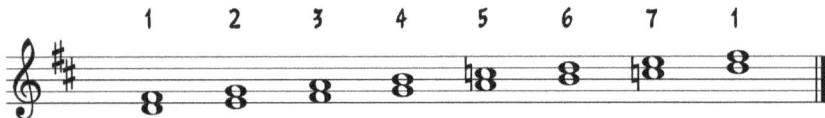

Again these are easy to work out if you already know the major scales and in turn the major-third intervals. All you need to do is to remember to flatten the seventh.

Additional Minor-Third

Here we will add the minor-third to the mix, which creates more interest again, although it is quite dissonant (more so than the seventh) so requires careful use.

Thirds With Minor-Third (Key Of 'C')

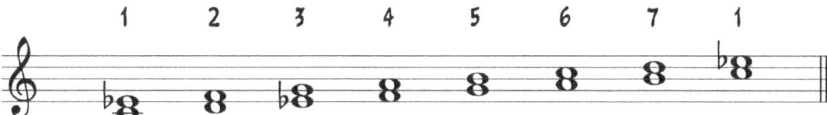

The minor-third is found within the minor pentatonic, minor blues scale and the major blues scales, so it can be used to good effect.

Thirds With Minor-Third (Key Of 'F')

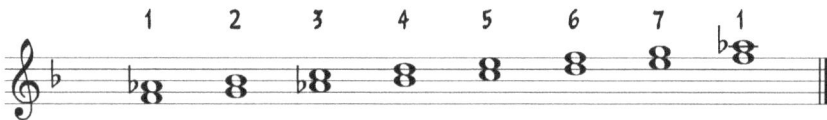

Thirds With Minor-Third (Key Of 'G')

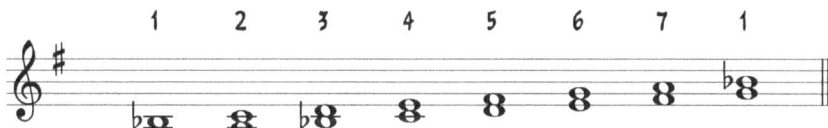

A run of thirds using the minor-third doesn't sound very good in a blues context (have a play around with it and see) but it works very well when used in conjunction with the major third. Switching between the major and minor thirds is a common thing in boogie. The run of thirds shown above do work well however when you combine them with the flat-seventh instead of the major.

Diminished Thirds (Key Of 'C')

I'm referring to this addition as 'diminished' as the two notes in question can be found within a diminished scale and would create a diminished chord if added to the root note. We are referring to the flat-third and flat-fifth.

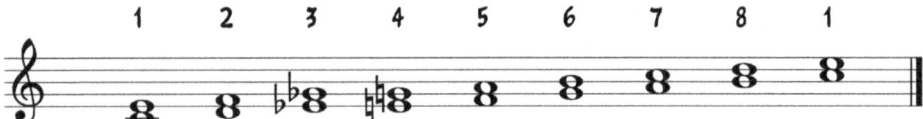

The two notes above have an addition as opposed to altering any of the existing notes in the scale. Both the flat-third and flat-fifth can be found within the minor-blues scale. The third and fifth still remain though, as they work very nicely with the flat-third and flat-fifth. The switching back and forth is a common blues thing, the dissonant sound of the flat-third/fifth resolving back to the major sound.

Diminished Thirds (Key Of 'F')

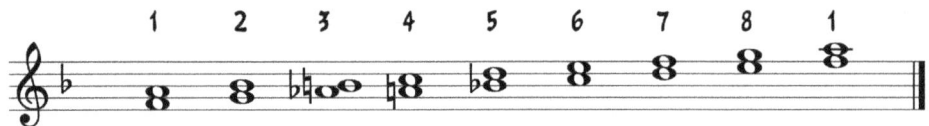

Diminished Thirds (Key Of 'G')

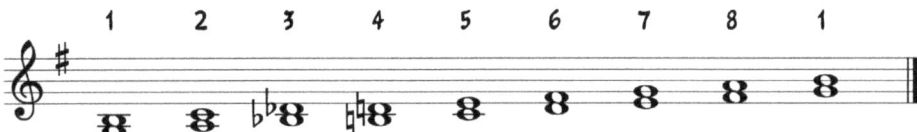

The following pages have the thirds shown in every key. Learning/practising them like this may be tiresome, but drilling them into your subconscious will help a great deal when improvising.

Note

In order to make them work better musically, they have been combined in two different combinations. The diminished with the seventh and the minor-third with the flat-seventh.

Thirds Practice 1

Thirds With Diminished And Flat-Seventh   (A To D)

A

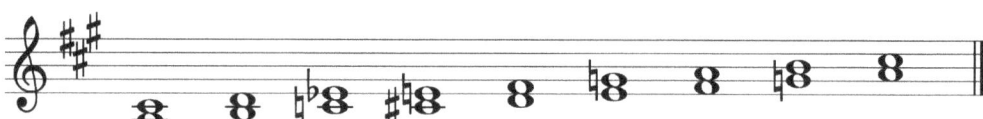

B♭

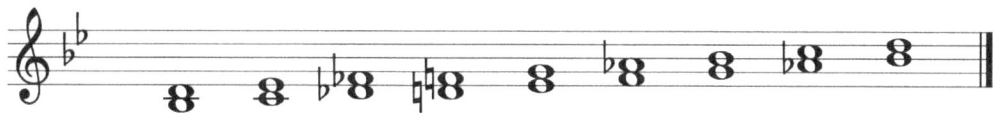

B

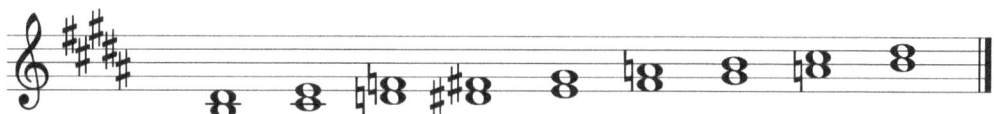

C

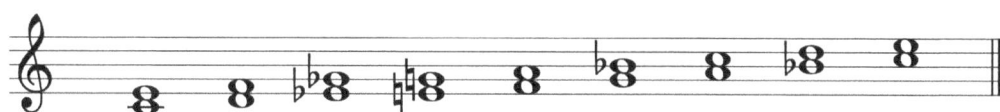

D♭

D

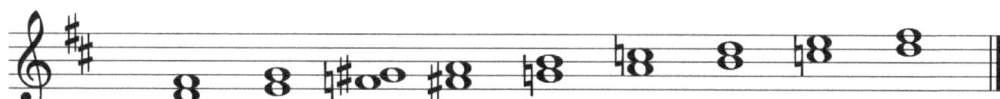

Thirds With Diminished And Flat-Seventh (E♭ To A♭)

E♭

E

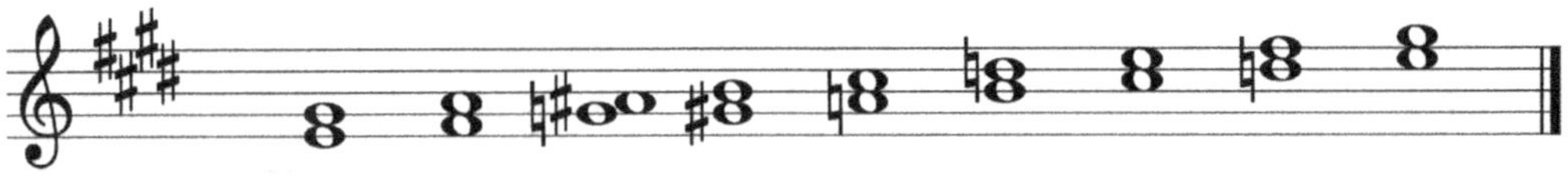

F

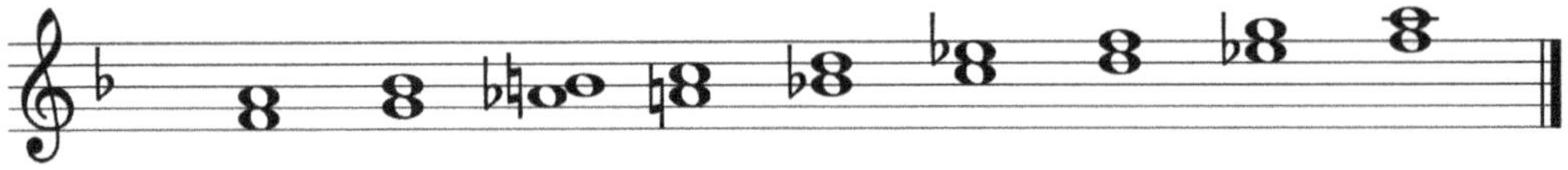

G♭

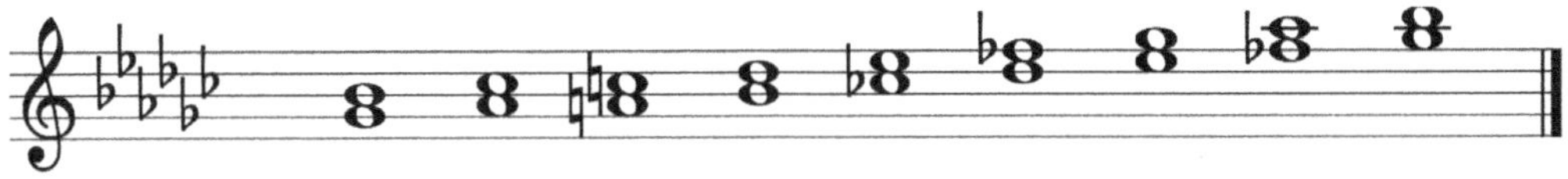

G

A♭

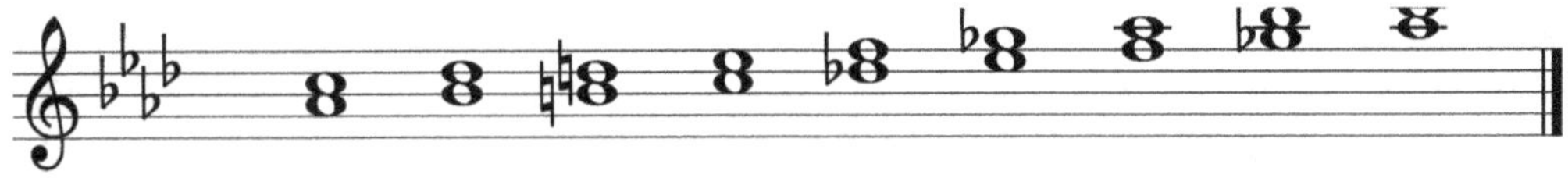

Thirds Practice 2

Thirds With Minor-Third and Flat-Seventh   (A To D)

A

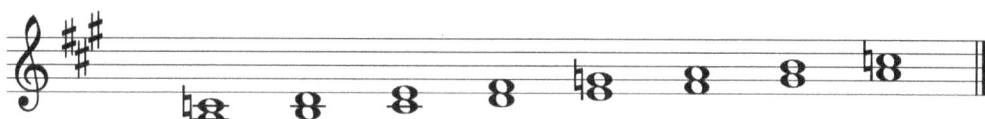

B♭

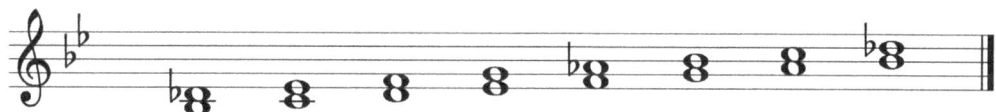

B

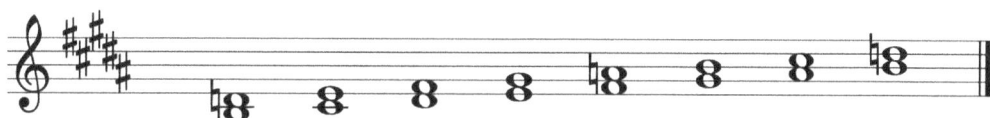

C

D♭

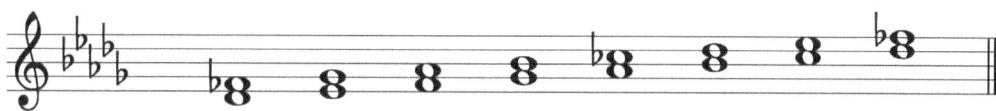

D

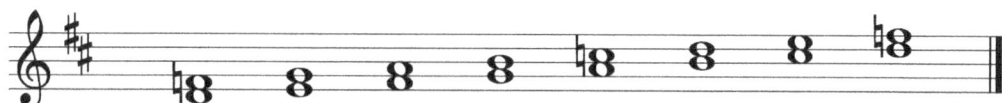

Thirds With Minor-Third and Flat-Seventh (E♭ To A♭)

E♭

E

F

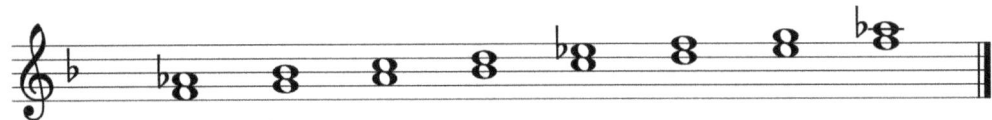

G♭

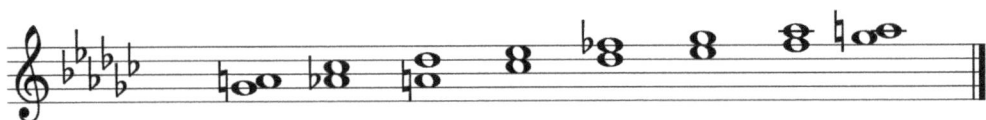

G

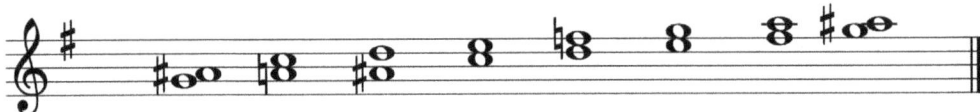

A♭

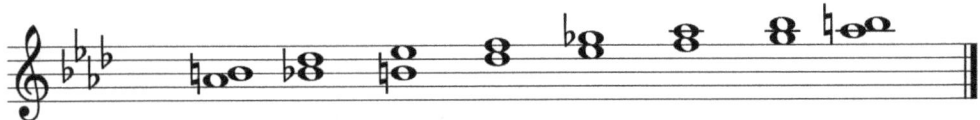

Runs With Thirds

One thing you can do with thirds is incorporate them into a run down the keyboard (Or alternatively, up the keyboard). This can be done in many ways, either completely straight (as shown below) or with a more up and down random movement even mixed in with other ideas/riffs.

1.

Built off the major scale with no alterations.

2.

Additional flat-third and flat-fifth.

3.

Using flat-third and flat-seventh.

4.

Using triplets timing.

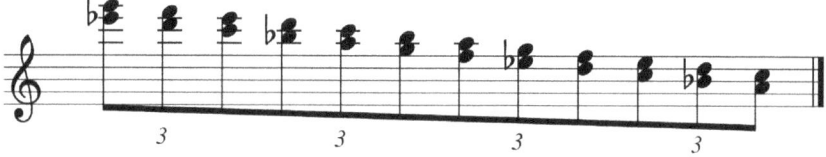

5.

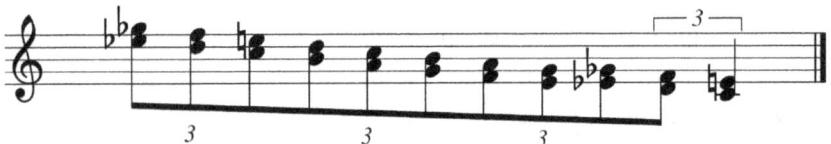

6.

Running downwards with additional upwards movement.

7.

A variation with a similar movement pattern.

8.

Repeating each third (played twice each).

9.

Varying the timing with some notes held longer, here with the third being tied between bars.

There are more riffs with thirds than you can sensibly put in any book, but we can take a look at some ideas that you can make use of, which will hopefully lead you to create ideas of your own.

1.

A mix of long and short notes.

2.

Add some triplets.

3.

You don't have to only use thirds, so mix them in with both chords or single note parts.

4.

Introduce tremolos on the longer notes. It's a great sound and also gives you a breath whilst playing.

5.

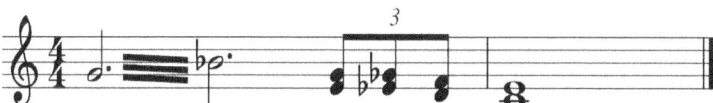

A common form of pattern sees you use a series of thirds that alternate with a single lower note below them.

6.

7.

Or... below has you using thirds in a more repetitive way.

8.

9.

10.

11.

Runaway Boogie

Creating Riffs From Thirds

The aim of this book is to help in improvising, so with this in mind, now would be a good time to have a play around with making riffs with thirds. This isn't meant to be a definitive list, but rather to prompt you into experimenting yourself and seeing what works and what doesn't, this is how we learn, trying things out for ourselves.

Keeping within '**C**' for simplicity we are going to walk through an improvisation in slow motion. Below we have some options to choose from again. You can start from anywhere, but music often starts within its chord tones, so that's a good place to begin.

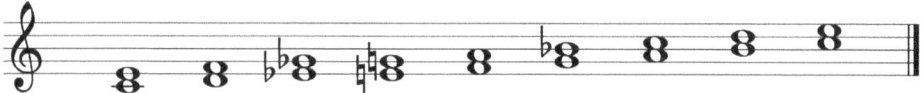

So with this in mind, choose a starting point. Below we are using the chord tones (root and third).

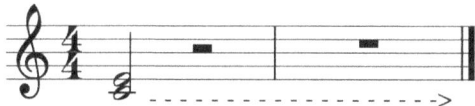

So now what...

Consider These Points

- Are you moving up or down?
- Jumping to another position?
- Moving slowly or fast?
- Using triplets?
- Using a tremolo or alternating pattern?

If you aren't sure where you want the music to go, just pick something or somewhere randomly, continue on and see where it takes you. Sometimes an improvisation can be average and another time it can spark something great. Naturally, like anything it gets better with practice, so it doesn't matter where it leads, the thing to do is just play.

So this is where we are starting...

We could move slowly and steady like this...

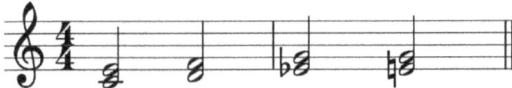

Or a little quicker...

If we choose the latter, what to play? We have no plan, so using some thirds close to the starting point we alternate up and down between them, simple enough.

Now what? There's still no plan, so we repeat the pattern for a moment before moving downwards, safely back to the chord tones we originally began with.

Alternatively, from this same starting point you might have felt like playing triplets instead.

Keeping it simple we move up again from the starting point.

What next? We could just play continuous triplets with the same notes over the whole bar.

Or relax the music at the end by slowing it down slightly with the longer note, and moving back to where we began with.

This is just to prompt you into playing around with improvising, now experiment with as many ideas as you can come up with. Some will be better than others, but that is how we learn.

Left-Hand Pattern 2

This left-hand pattern is very much like a walking bass-line except that it's cut short and steps back on itself. Although it feels similar to play, it's probably a fair bit easier.

12-bar Practice Example

On bars nine and ten of a twelve-bar, you could always swap out this pattern for a simple alternating octave using the chord root note. It's optional of course, but you could throw it in sometimes to break up the monotony.

Variation

The next song example uses this variation throughout. You could just use the main pattern if you wish, or switch it about. It's in '**G**' and continues with the thirds along with some single note twiddly bits in triplets, which we will have a good look at later on.

Boogie The Third

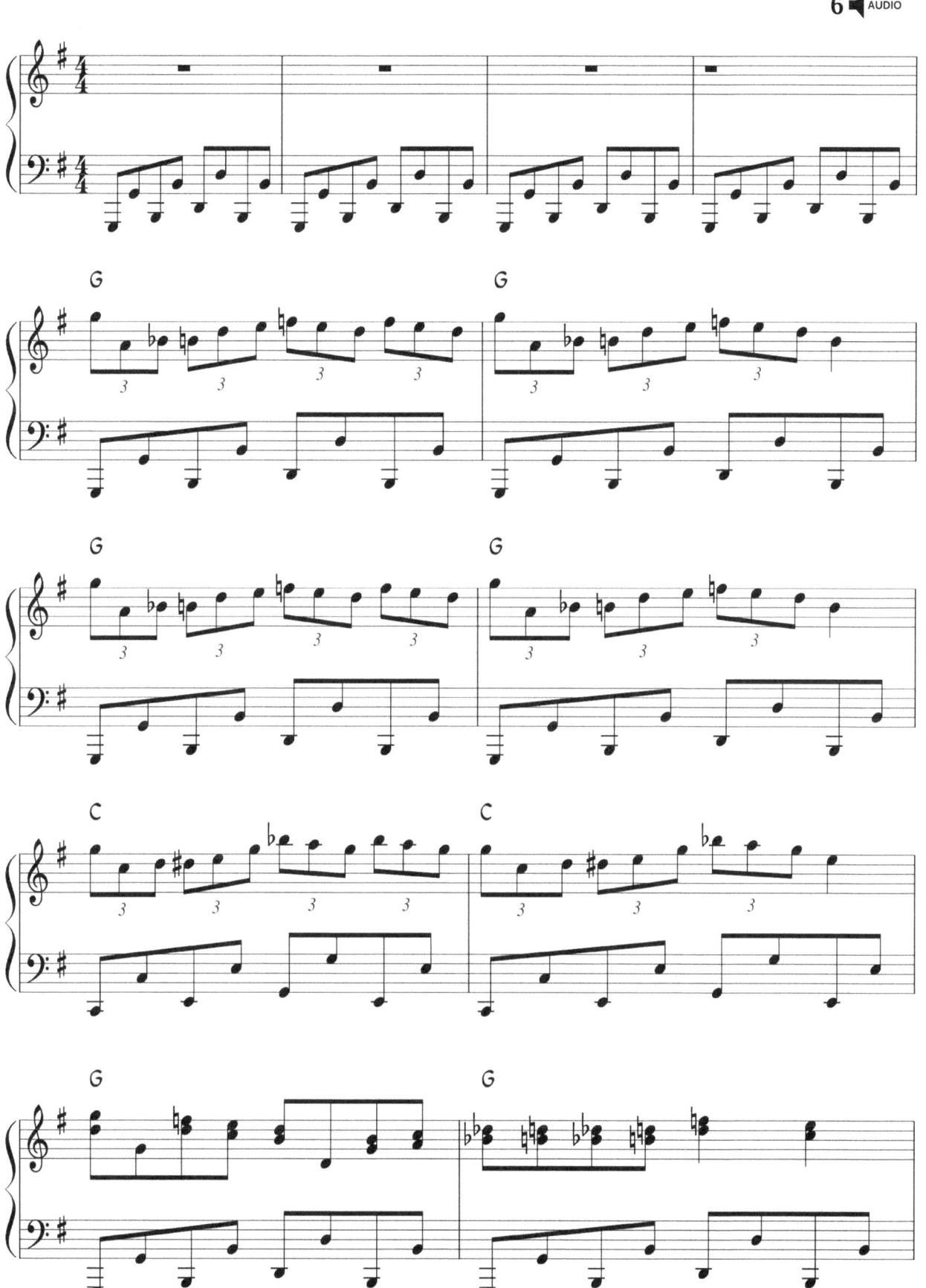

Using Sixths

As well as using thirds, it's a good idea to get used to playing around with sixths as well, as these intervals are used fairly often with the right-hand.

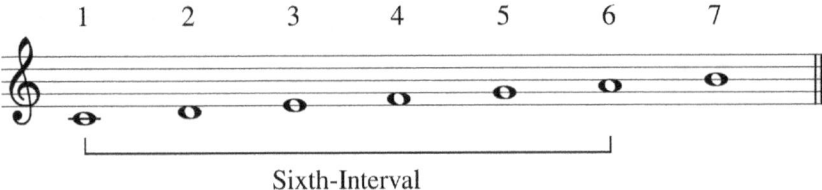

Sixth-Interval

As shown in the diagram above, a sixth is two notes that are six intervals apart. The second note is five steps (through the scale) higher than the first.

Relationship To Thirds

Something you may or may not have noticed is that a sixth has a lot in common with a third, in-fact they use exactly the same notes, but they have been inverted/swapped around.

Sixth

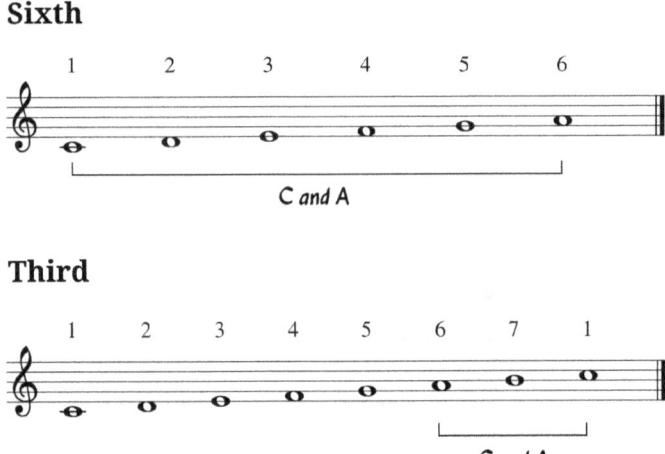

The relationship between them doesn't have a huge significance here, but it does help understand and learn them. Once you know the thirds off by heart then it's easier to get your head around the sixths, as you can see if it's the correct note or not, as it has to match up to a third interval. Any general knowledge always helps with working things out.

Sixth Options In 'C'

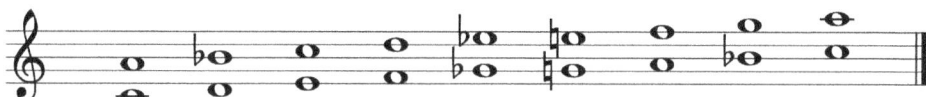

Here we have sixths you might use. You can see that it's been altered from the standard major scale as per-usual. We've omitted the major-seventh in favour of the flat/dominant seventh, and included the flat-third and flat-fifth, otherwise it's from a **'C'** major scale.

Example Patterns

So that's a few ideas that you can use with sixths. Unlike thirds, they aren't quite as flexible, by this I mean that they are best used in-conjunction with other ideas, as steps within something larger, it's difficult to create much using only sixths alone. So now we have to put it into some real life context and experiment with different ways of using these within an actual boogie-woogie piece. You can use the next example pieces to practice using the sixth interval.

Boogie On The Six

Six Times Boogie

The Scales Behind The Music

The many riffs, licks, and melody lines you hear in boogie-woogie are obviously made up of notes, but being a blues based style, they tend to come from a specific source, or at least the majority of the time.

Boogie-woogie piano is a form of blues or at least a specific sub-set of it, and as such it's created from the same material, being the major/minor blues scales. These are modified pentatonic scales and are often considered to not even be real by traditional music theory, but their use over all these years tends to tell a different story.

Interesting Note

The major-blues scale is strangely not as well known as the minor-blues, which is often referred to as the '*blues scale*' as if there is only one. But it's a very important scale to know for boogie-woogie.

Reasons To Learn The Blues Scale

- Understanding how various riffs and melodies are created.

- Aid in transposing the music into different keys.

- Help in creating/improvising your own music.

The thought of scales can turn some people off, and I can understand that, but if you feel that way, please persevere. They are very important to know if you want to go beyond sheet-music and improvise your own boogie-woogie (and that's where the real fun is).

Bear in mind that although they are important, there's no need to punish yourself with endless monotonous practice, it's this that can put people off (although if it doesn't, by all means practise as much as you want). I'd suggest instead to practice a little on a regular basis (every day if you can) but just for a little while, so as not to drive you insane. Keep doing this and in time it will add up and make a huge difference to your knowledge and skills.

- **Understanding how riffs are created**

With knowledge of the scales that are used you will be able to understand how the different pattern/riffs within songs that you learn (from sheet music or by ear) were created. This will help you learn the music itself, as once you know that a particular part or run down the keyboard uses a specific set of notes from a scale, it then becomes easier to learn, play and even remember.

- **Aid in transposing the music into different keys**

Knowing the scales will also allow you to dissect a pattern/riff and think of it in terms of its origin within a scale (i.e. the root, third, or fifth etc.) Once you can do that, when you want to play the same thing in a different key you will then know which scale intervals it was created from, which in turn allows you to re-create it in another key. This really saves a lot of time, thought and effort.

- **Help in creating/improvising your own music**

If you are creating your own boogie-woogie music, knowing the scales will help endlessly in being able to improvise new parts, or even modify old ones that you already know. Improvisation isn't magic, it's just using a wealth of stored/practised knowledge that you have picked up and then implementing it at will. Sometimes it isn't perfect, sometimes you get something great, but it's all based on what you have picked up over time.

> First off we need to have a quick look at the scales in question (if you already know them then that's great). On the following pages we have both the pentatonic and the blues scales (basically a modified pentatonic) shown in every key. This is followed by a few suggestions on how you might practise them, and then we look at how you can use them.

The Pentatonic Scales

First we have the pentatonic scales, they consist of five notes (hence the 'pent' part of the name). This won't be the main focus here as they're related to the blues scales (being what the blues scales are built from). There is only one note between them, but that note does make a difference, so when the pentatonic is used (or that extra note is omitted) you do have a different sound, so it's useful to remember. And of course the scale is used in other styles as well.

Major-Pentatonic

The major-pentatonic is created from the following...

- Root
- Second
- Third
- Fifth
- Sixth

Minor-Pentatonic

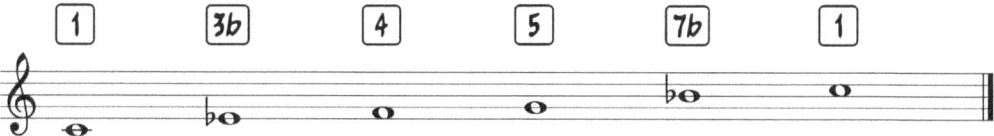

The minor-pentatonic is created from the following...

- Root
- Flat-Third
- Fourth
- Fifth
- Flat-Seventh

The Blues Scales

The blues scales are essentially the pentatonic scales with an additional note. This might not sound like a major difference but the extra note (the so called 'blue notes') goes a long way to create some of the magic, it's surprising how much difference one note actually makes. The major-blues scale is not as well known (shockingly even unheard of by many experienced players) but it certainly does exist and is quite important to know.

Major-Blues

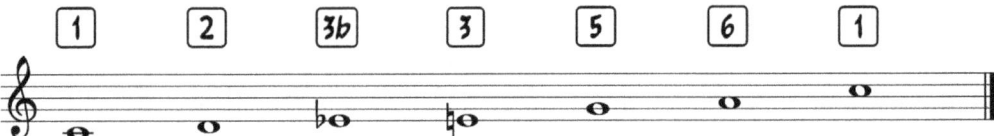

The major-blues scale is created from the following...

- Root
- Second
- Flat-Third
- Third
- Fifth
- Sixth

Minor-Blues

The minor-blues scale is created from the following...

- Root
- Flat-Third
- Fourth
- Flat-Fifth
- Fifth
- Flat-Seventh

Major-Blues Scales

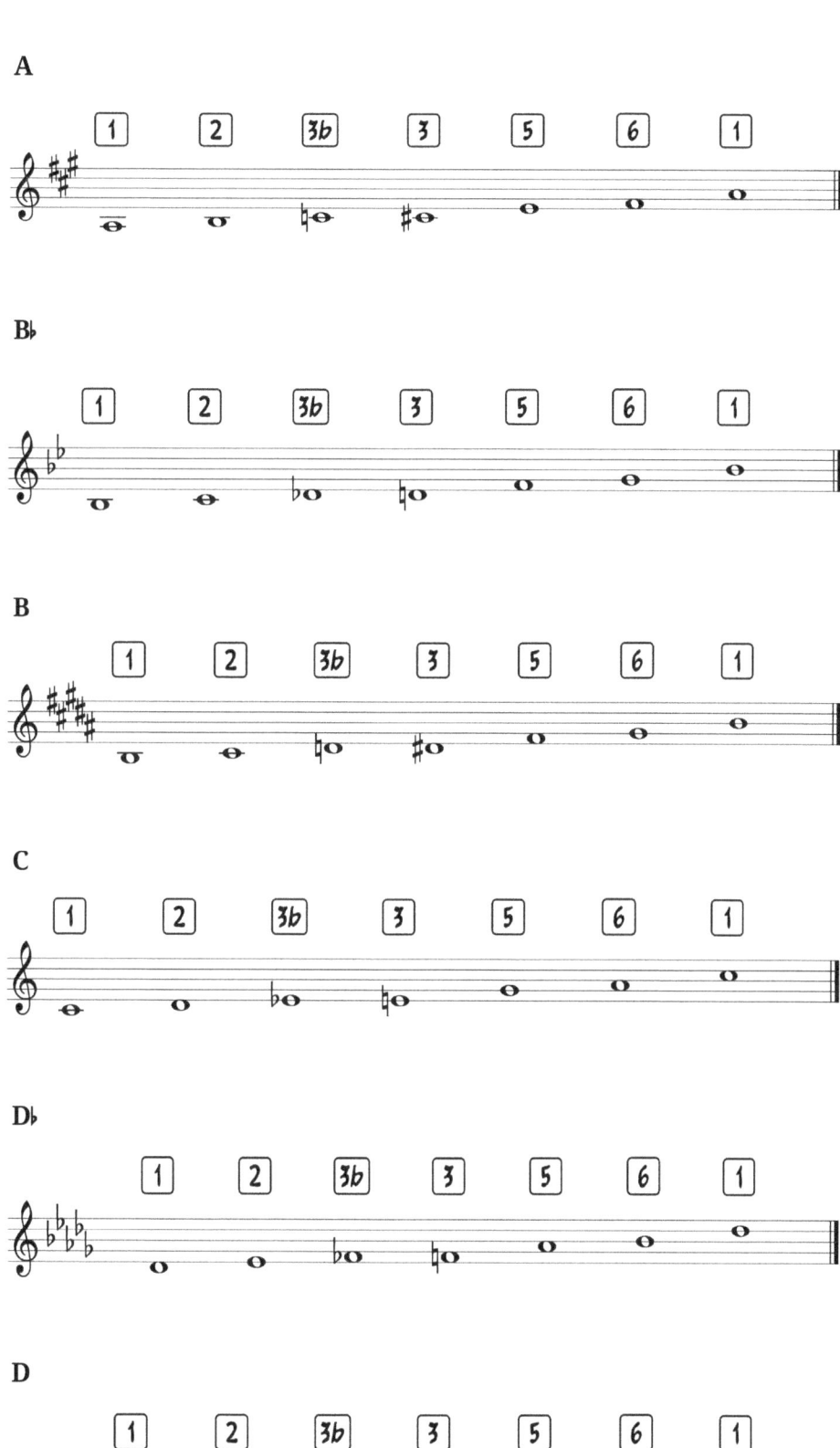

Major-Blues Scales

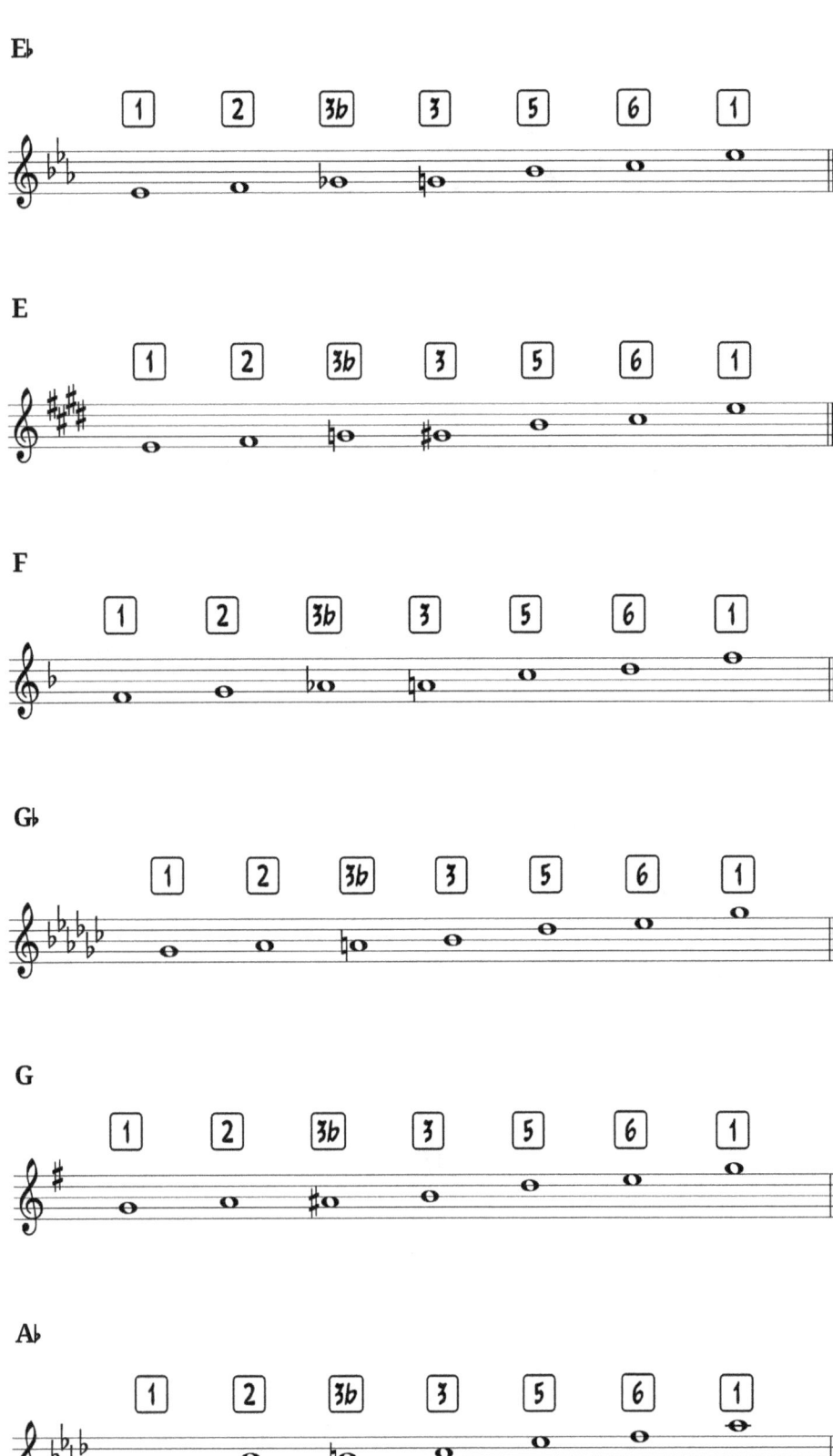

346

Minor-Blues Scales

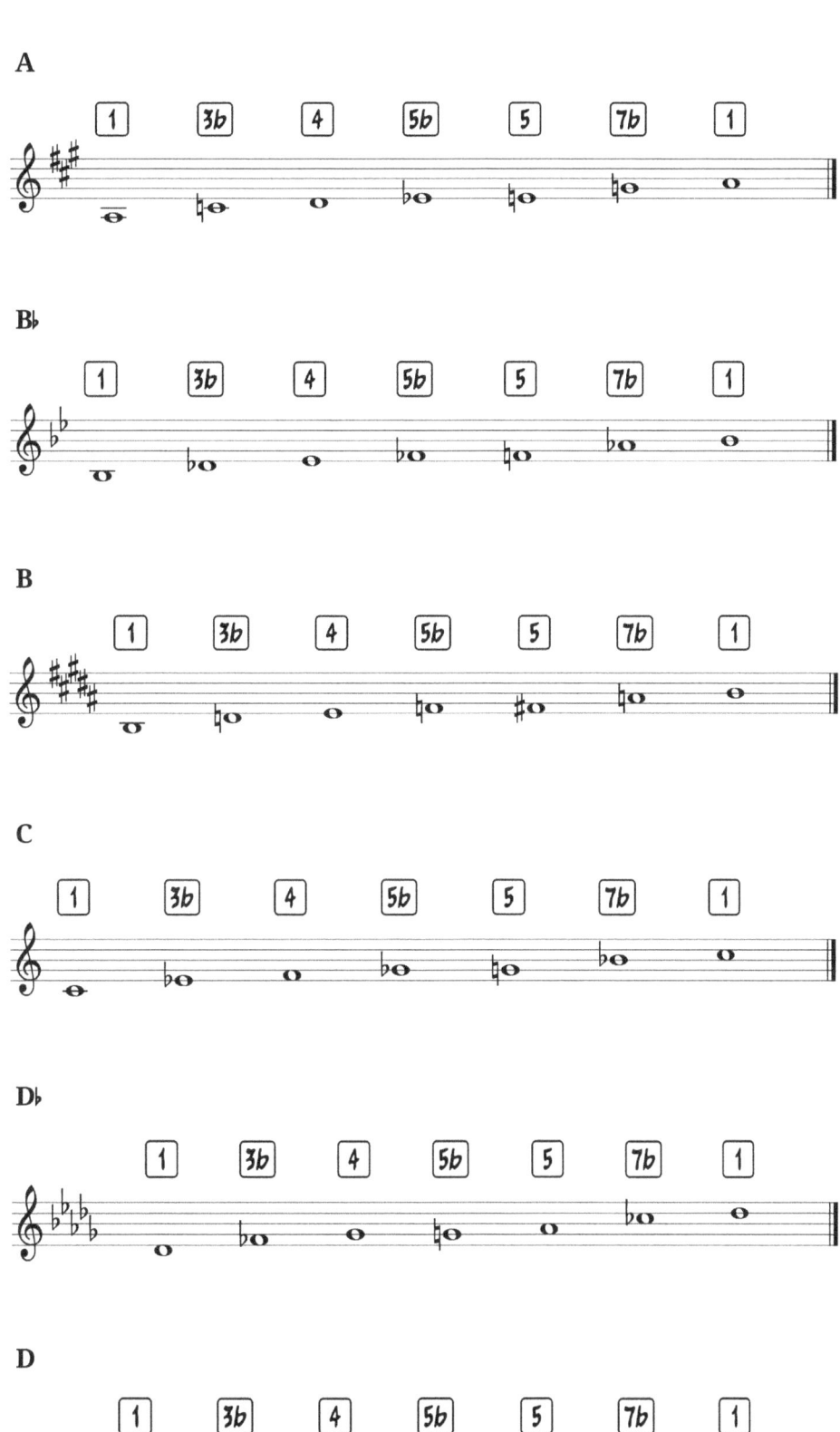

Minor-Blues Scales

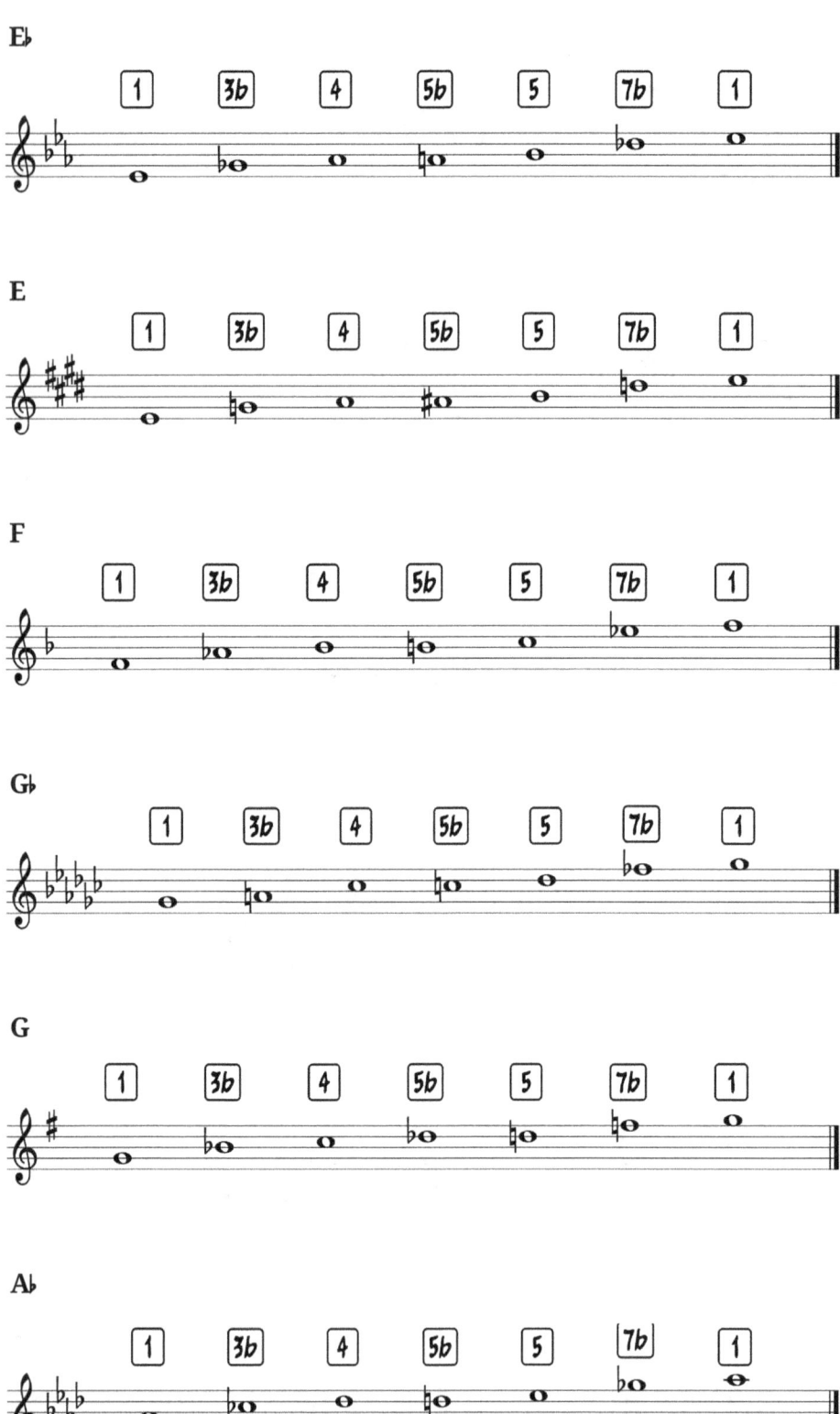

Relative Minors

Just as with the regular major-scales, the major pentatonic/major blues scales have relative minors (the minor pentatonic/minor blues scales). A relative minor scale uses exactly the same notes as the major scale it relates to, but with a different root note.

The sixth degree of the major scale dictates its relative minor. The sixth degree of '**C**' major is a '**A**', therefore the relative minor of '**C**' major-blues is '**A**' minor-blues.

'C' Major Blues Scale

'A' Minor Blues Scale

You can see above how these two related scales use the same notes. Now while knowing the relative minor relationship doesn't make a great deal of difference to your playing, knowledge of what you are dealing with always helps. One benefit is that once you know the notes to one scale, you actually also know them for its relative scale.

It's important to differentiate the major from the minor blues scale. Although the notes of 'A-minor blues' are the same as 'C-major blues' you're not playing 'A-minor blues' over that 'C' chord, it's 'C-major blues'.

Making this distinction is important, always consider them separate whilst practicing, it will help no end, not to mention being the correct way of thinking.

How To Practice

Getting started practising these scales is simple enough, although I'm not going to include endless and endless pages of scales here, but we will have a few suggestions on how you might practise them.

You will notice that I'm not including the left-hand here. Although it's normal practice to go over scales using both hands on the piano, in boogie-woogie this isn't really an efficient use of your time. The left-hand is generally (ninety-nine percent of the time) doing its own thing, normally a repetitive rhythmic pattern that will not benefit from endless practising of scales. The right-hand of course is different, and knowing these scales is very important. By all means, feel free to practise them with the left-hand too, it's just that it won't benefit you so much for this particular style.

Practice Over One Octave

Practice Over Two Octaves

Practice Over Three Octaves

Major

Minor

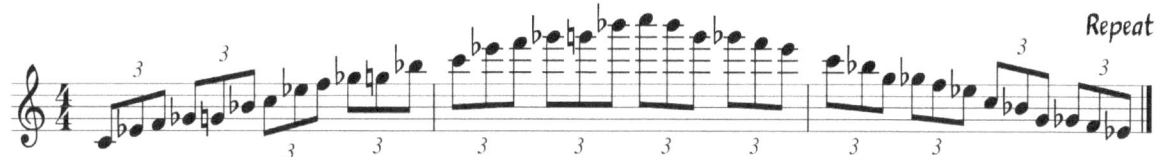

If a scale is new to you, then I would start by just practising over a single octave, run up the scale and then run down repeatedly. This is probably the best way to initially get the scale into your head. Once you are happy with it, you can practice over longer distances, two or three octaves worth perhaps, and from there even divide the scale up into patterns.

Different Keys

Naturally not everything is in the key of '**C**', so you will need to learn these in various keys. You can either try and learn them all at the same time, or just choose the ones that correspond to the particular keys you are concentrating on at the moment. Don't feel that you should practise it everything at once and know it instantly, take your time and go at your own speed.

Pentatonic Scales

The pentatonic scales are in essence the basis of the blues scales. Although they are important to know generally, I wouldn't necessarily over practice them for boogie-woogie use, but rather be aware that you can omit that single note and be within them. That's just a suggestion to save time, feel free to practise them separately if you wish.

The Scales Within

As an example of how the blues scales create the riffs and patterns in boogie-woogie piano, we are going to highlight a few sections of the next exercise piece to show how they consist (at least partly) of these scales. I'd skip ahead and take a quick look of the example first perhaps and then come back here. It's quite simple, but think about how some notes are from within the blues scales as you play, and the different intervals used.

Take the first bar, you will find that it consists entirely of notes from the major-blues scale.

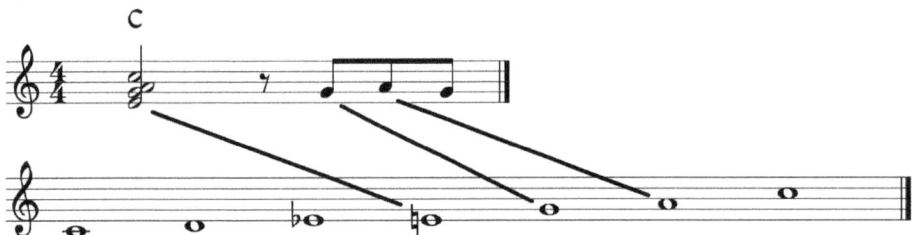

Or here on the 'IV' chord, it is created predominantly from the 'F' major-blues scale (with the exception of E-flat), which is found in the minor-blues scale.

In case you are wondering how the E-natural fits in here (as it isn't found in either the major or minor blues scale of the 'F' chord) it does so in two ways.

The **E**-note can be found within the '**C**' major-blues scale and seeing as that is the '**I**' chord in this key, it will work over all the chords, '**I**', '**IV**' and '**V**'.

The E-note also works as it comes from the following chord of the next bar, so it leads into it. This is a common thing and can be heard being done quite often.

Scales Within One

Scales Within Two

The following is another example of how the music is formed from the blues scales. Using a variation of a commonly used riff, we can see how it is based around both of the blues scales. Again it is quite easy, but think about how some notes come from within the blues scales as you play and the different intervals used.

Major-Blues Scale

You can see how every note but one, is found in the major blues scale. The exception being the B-flat.

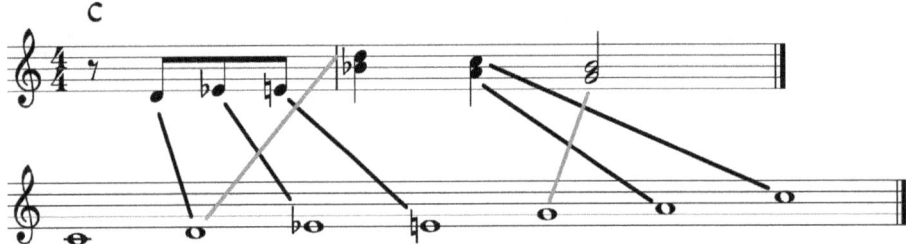

Minor-Blues Scale

Here you can see that the B-flat used that was missing from the major-blues scale can be found within the minor-blues scale, along with a few others as well.

The scales work either singularly or when combined. When used in combination there are only three notes left that aren't available (or at least need extreme care).

- Flat-ninth
- Flat-sixth
- Major-seventh

Scales Within Two

Which Scale?

Knowing some scales is one thing, actually doing something constructive with them is something else. The aim of the game with boogie-woogie should be to learn how to improvise. You do this by learning a selection of riffs, creating a palette of possibilities that you can drop into when you feel fit, but you also do this by tapping into the notes from the scales that suit the music.

For the most part here we are going to be playing around using single note lines (as in only using a single note at a time) as opposed to more complex stuff. Call them twiddly bits if you like (it's how I refer to this kind of boogie stuff anyway, not exactly a technical term, but it fits).

What Scale To Use

What am I talking about here? Well this is the strange thing about blues music which you may well know. Whatever key you are playing in, the blues scales of that key will work over all three chords of a twelve-bar blues. This goes against traditional music theory and so in theory it shouldn't work, but nobody told the original blues masters this, so it definitely does work, it's all part of the magic.

You can of course also use the scales from the individual chords that you are on also. So in the key of '**C**' you could use the '**C**' blues scales over all three chords, or use the scales from that specific chord. The chart below shows which scales are useable over which chords.

Scale Usable Over Chords

Chord	Usable Scale
I	I
IV	I or IV
V	I or V

Options For scales Over Chords

Key	I Chord	IV Chord	V Chord
A	A	A or D	A or E
B♭	B♭	B♭ or E♭	B♭ or F
B	B	B or E	B or G♭
C	C	C or F	C or G
D♭	D♭	D♭ or G♭	D♭ or A♭
D	D	D or G	D or A
E♭	E♭	E♭ or A♭	E♭ or B♭
E	E	E or A	E or B
F	F	F or B♭	F or C
G♭	G♭	G♭ or B	G♭ or D♭
G	G	G or C	G or D
A♭	A♭	A♭ or D♭	A♭ or E♭

Which Ones To Use?

So you have your options, but which ones are best to use? (Bear in mind, here we are only talking about single note twiddly bits, not more complex patterns made up of intervals and chords). So generally speaking you can't go wrong using the base 'I' key as this always sounds great, it's perhaps what's used more than anything else. The way the 'I' chord scales work over all the chords is a big part of the blues sound. The 'IV' and 'V' scales can of course be used over their matching chords, but can be a little trickier to fit in well. It's possible to transpose the same pattern used on the 'I' chord to the other chords, as there aren't any rules as such, nobody has written a rule book that must be obeyed, so learn the scales and experiment. What is learnt in this manner goes deeper than that which you are taught.

> The following page has examples of how the scales sound over the chords. The first uses the 'I' chords scale over all three chords, the other uses the scale matching each of the individual chords.

The 'I' Minor-Blues Scale Over All Chords

Matching Minor-Blues Scale Over Each Chord

Twiddly Boogie Riffs

Knowledge of scales helps in general playing/improvising regardless of what you are doing, but the easiest or best place to start is with single note twiddly riffs. Keeping with a single note pattern is less to think about to begin with, plus it's very fairly common thing for the right-hand anyway.

Improvising isn't magic, and certainly in the simple form we are doing here (single notes). We are taking a set of notes (from a scale or two) and rearranging them into a different order that will hopefully sound musical.

There are different ways you could approach beginning this, but we are going to try to split it up into different ideas, the first of which is splitting the scale into groupings. This is just a case of only using a number of the notes from the scale at a time (say three or maybe four) and creating a repeating pattern from them only. You might then move to a different position within the scale and use a different set of notes. Ultimately you won't think in these terms once you are more practised, but it's a good way to set limits in order to make it easier to do something that's new to you.

We are going to split the scales up into three, four and five note groupings, which within each you can come up with various combinations of notes with different timings/rhythmic ideas. Doing this in stages like this will help you get comfortable with the scales, getting the physical patterns committed to your muscle memory and easier to recall. The more notes in the group, the more complex the possibilities are, gradually increasing until you use all/any available notes to improvise with and are completely free. But remember that the simple smaller patterns that use just a few notes are always used, sometimes less is definitely more.

Minor Blues Scale

Three Note Grouping Ideas

Here the minor-blues scale has been split and grouped into only three notes. This is commonly used in a triplet form as shown here. The twelve-bar example is just for practice purposes, you wouldn't want to repeat the same pattern for this long in reality.

Practice Twelve-Bar Example

Four Note Grouping Examples

Three notes is fine at times but a little limiting, so now we will step it up to four notes. Below are a few examples of patterns created using the minor-blues scale. Again, this is only a tiny sample of the possibilities.

1.

2.

3.

4.

5.

6.

7.

8.

Practice Twelve-Bar Example

A short example of some patterns built around four note groupings using the minor-blues scale.

Experiment yourself by improvising patterns using four note groupings over a twelve-bar. Sticking to only four notes is a little limiting, but it's good practice. Feel free to try it in as many keys as you wish.

Improvise Over Twelve-Bars

Five Note Grouping Examples

Here we have some examples that are using five notes from the minor-blues scale.

1.

2.

3.

4.

5.

6.
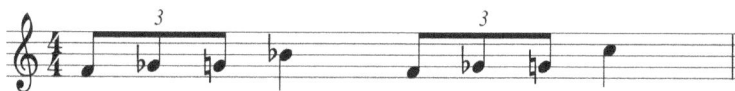

7.

8.

Practice Twelve Bar Example

A short example of some patterns built around five note groupings using the minor-blues scale.

Experiment yourself by improvising patterns using five note groupings over a twelve-bar. Sticking to five notes is still limiting ultimately, but it's good practice. Feel free to try it in as many keys as you wish.

Improvise Over Twelve-Bars

Minor-Blues Patterns

The examples below allow for the use of all the notes within the minor-blues scale.

1.

2.

3.

4.

5.

6.

7.

8.

Major Blues Groupings

Don't neglect the major-blues scale as it is an important aspect of boogie-woogie playing, so with that in mind let's run over the same idea with the major-blues scale.

Three Note Grouping Ideas

These are all created from the same major-blues scale, merely different combinations of notes in different orders.

Practice Twelve-Bar Example

Four Note Grouping Examples

Here we have a few examples of four note groupings created from the major-blues scale.

Practice Twelve-Bar Example

A short example of some patterns built around four note groupings using the major-blues scale.

Experiment yourself by improvising patterns using four note groupings over a twelve-bar. Remember not to limit yourself to just one key.

Improvise Over Twelve-Bars

Five Note Grouping Examples

Here we have some examples that are using five notes from the major-blues scale.

Practice Twelve-Bar Example

A short twelve-bar example using some patterns built around five note groupings from the major-blues scale.

Experiment yourself by improvising patterns using five note groupings over a twelve-bar. Feel free to try it in as many keys as you wish.

Improvise Over Twelve-Bars

Full Major-Blues Patterns

The examples below allow for the full use of all the notes within the major-blues scale.

Notes On Following Song Examples

The next two song examples incorporate a lot of single note twiddly bits like we have been looking at, but they differ in a couple of ways.

The first one primarily plays around within the minor-blues scale, while the second is mostly the major-blues scales (with the odd exceptions in places). You should be able to hear the difference in the sound they create, even though they are in different keys.

The other difference is that the second song goes further and also incorporates chords rather than being singular notes throughout, and it does this in two ways.

1.

Using chords within actual riffs built from chords rather than only using single notes.

2.

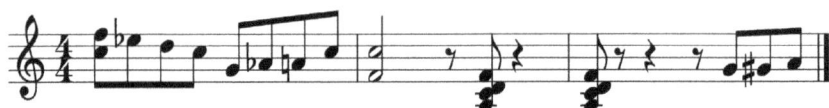

Switching between twiddly single note sections and rhythmic chord parts. This could be like above, where the change is frequent, switching every couple of bars. Or you could have twelve bars of twiddly patterns and then twelve bars of rhythmic chord parts before going back to twiddly stuff again.

Play through the song examples but as you do, think about what the notes are, or rather where they came from, how they fit within the scales we have looked at. When you are done, perhaps play around with them, alter parts or create new parts along the same lines that would fit with the existing music.

Twiddly Boogie Minor

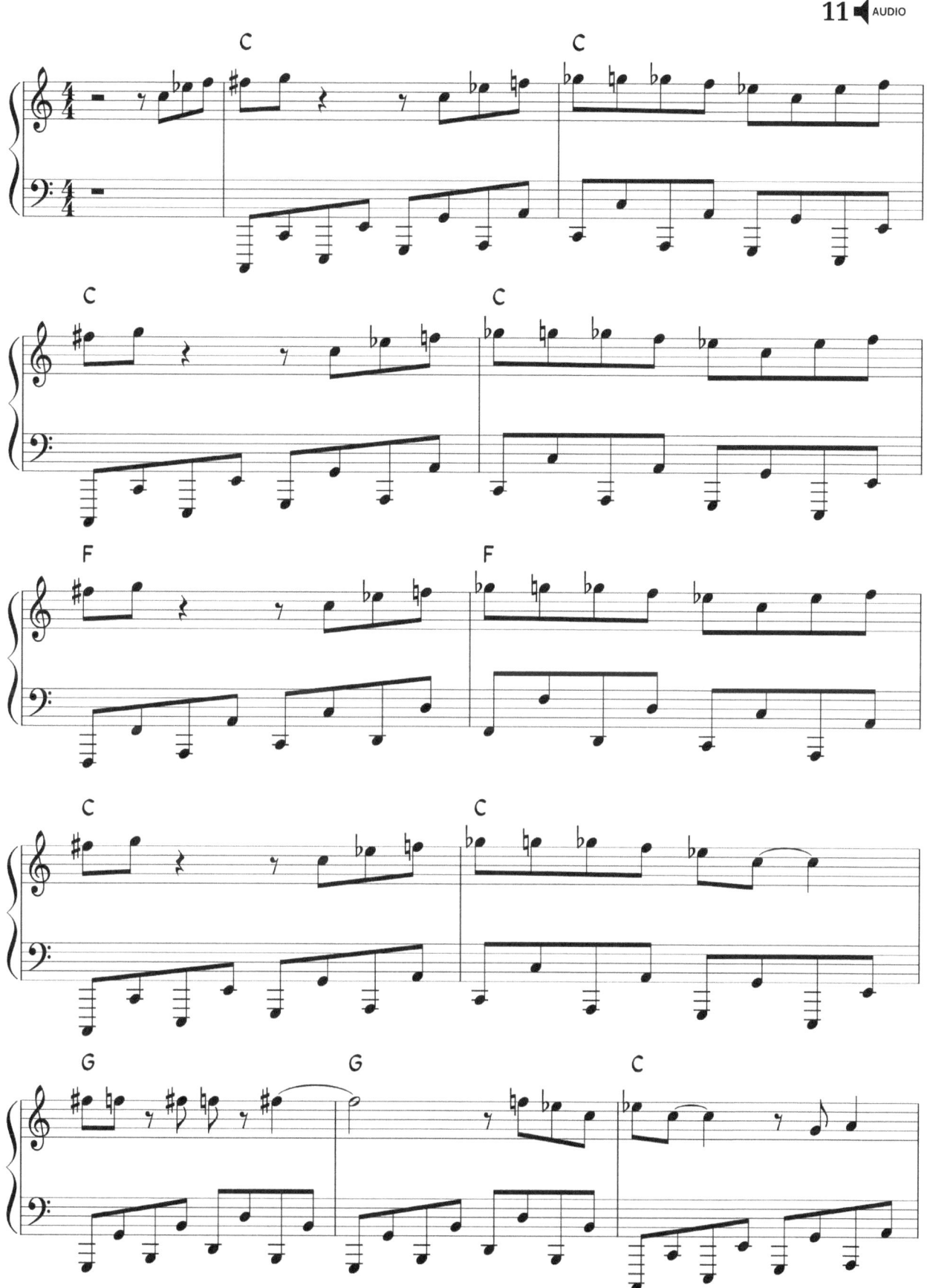

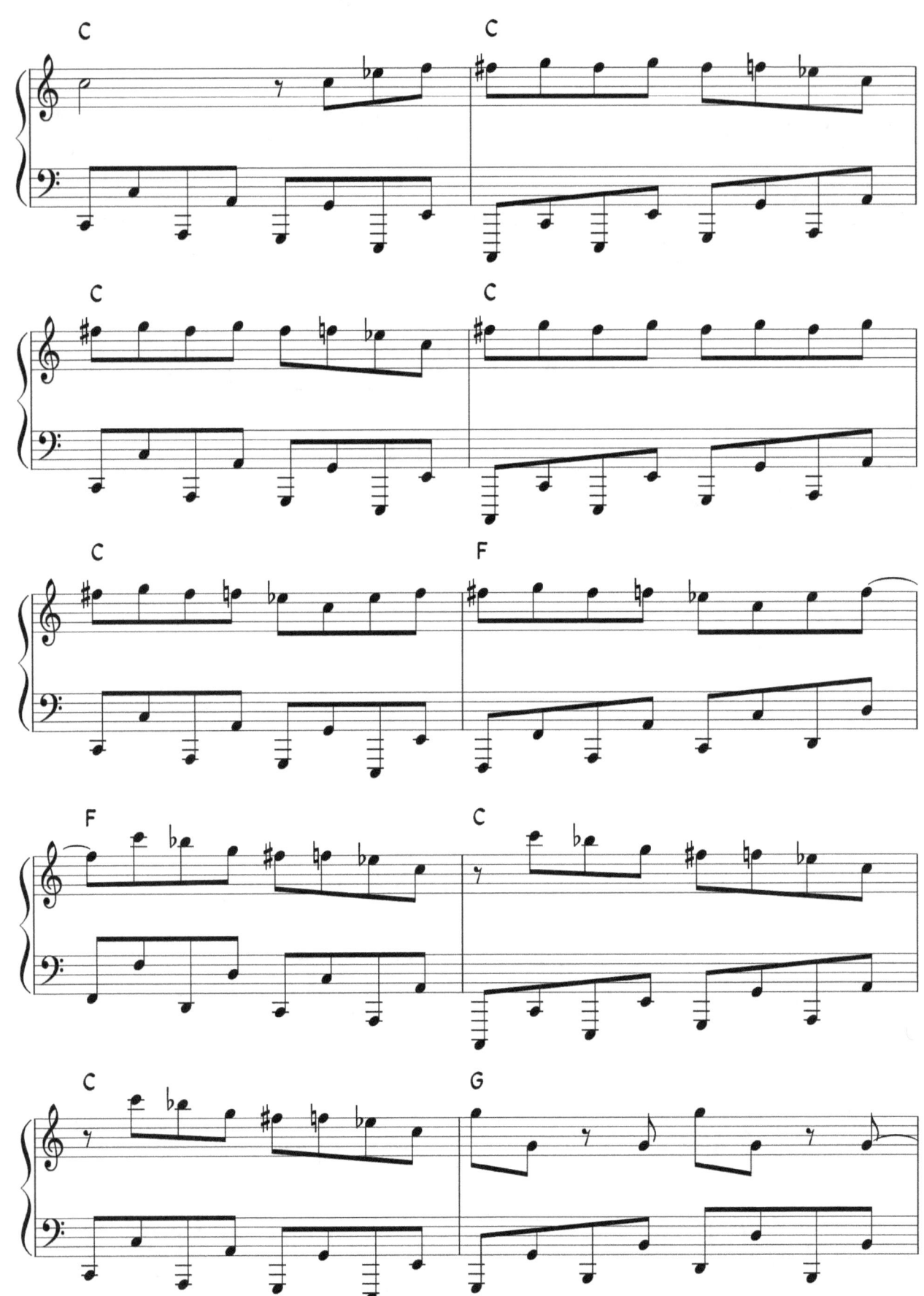

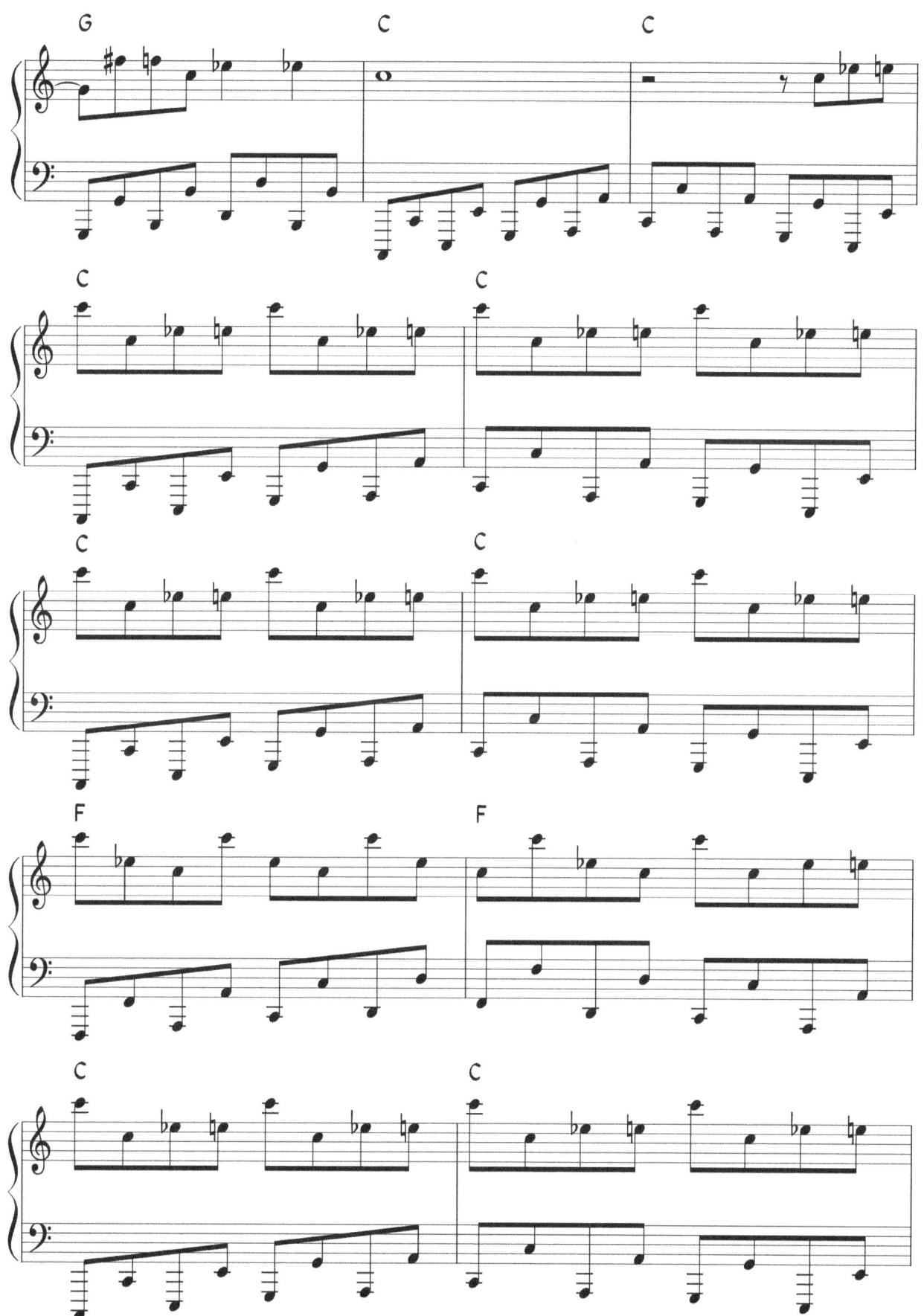

Twiddly Boogie Major

Creating Twiddly Riffs

We've looked at the scales commonly used along with some example riffs, we've also had a couple of song examples based mainly on either minor or major scales. If this is new to you then hopefully it will have given you some ideas for improvising. Admittedly it's hardly exhaustive as there are many styles of play and far more riffs and ideas than can be fitted into any book, but it's a start.

Between both the minor and major blues scales we actually have the majority of the notes available to us.

Combined Blues Scales In 'C'

You may notice that there aren't that many of the notes missing, only three to be exact.

Missing Notes

This isn't to say that the two scales combine well necessarily, they do and they don't. If you play around with the combination above you'll find that some combination of notes work okay, others sound quite rough, experimentation is the best way to learn. An easier way to begin to combine the two is to use them separately, but to flow from one to another.

Some Possible Options

1. Start in major-blues and swap to minor
2. Start with minor-blues and end in major
3. Start in major, swap to minor and back to major
4. Start in minor, swap to major and then back to minor
5. Start with a blues scale and end with a pentatonic
6. Start within a pentatonic scale and end in a blues scale

Major To Minor

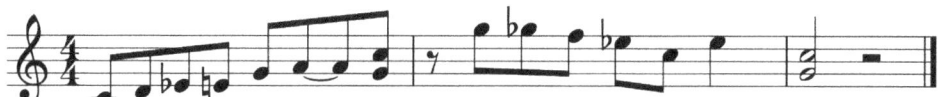

Minor To Major

Major To Minor And Back To Major

Minor To Major And Back To Minor

Blues Scale To Pentatonic

Pentatonic To Blues Scale

New From Old

If you are new to improvising then the best advice I can give is to just have a go, play something, play anything, but play something. We have looked at some of the tools that you can use, so it's a matter of getting stuck in and seeing what you come up with. It's just a matter of time, patients and of course lots of practice.

The simplest place to start is perhaps taking an existing pattern or riff and play around with it, altering it into something new. Below is what may be a familiar pattern.

Initial Pattern One

Now you could take this and alter it in many ways. Changing parts, shortening it, lengthening it, repeating sections. Next we'll look at some examples of what we could potentially do with this pattern to alter it.

Example. 1

Here we've taken the very first part and disregarded the rest, creating something new from what we already have.

Example. 2

We could make slight alterations to this to change it further. Here we have simply repeated the last notes.

Example. 3

This adds a little to the second half/repeat. It still uses the same notes as the original pattern, they're just rearranged.

Example. 4

Here the second bar moves more like the original, but instead of continuing downwards it moves back up.

Example. 5

The last bar is closer to the original, but ends higher with the tied notes of longer duration.

Example. 6

Here we change the timing/feel by switching to using triplets.

Example. 7

Now we have changed the initial three notes into triplets, which also moves them along the timeline.

Example. 8

Moving back towards the original, instead of repeating, it continues in a downward direction.

Example. 9

A slight variation that uses the flat-third and flat-fifth.

Example. 10

Here it moves down further, still using mostly thirds.

Example. 11

Losing the flat-fifth this time, the last bar repeats the same pattern of the flat-third moving to the third. It is also busier than previously as it doesn't have the rest at the end.

Example. 12

This time the second bar moves up to include the flat-seventh and also ends higher with the fifth and root.

Here we have another pattern to play around with and create something new. This time it's using only single notes.

Initial Pattern Two

Now we can look at ways to make something new out of the source material, using the same ideas, removing parts, repeating parts and adding something new here and there.

Example. 1

First we have taken the pattern and removed a lot of it, keeping the first five notes and then repeating them again, the extra end note gives it some finality.

Example. 2

Here we have taken the first example and added an ending that is similar in fashion to the original.

Example. 3

Now we have added an extra fill note to the second bar with a variation of example two on the end.

Example. 4

This time it has been shortened considerably by removing the whole of the last bar.

Example. 5

Here we have repeated the triplet part, playing it again in the third bar with a few extra notes to finish.

Example. 6

This time we have made even more of the triplet pattern and repeated it right across the two bars.

Example. 7

Here we use the double triplet part but then revert to the same last bar as the original pattern.

Example. 8

Now we have removed the triplets but retained the notes from the triplet part (changing the timing). The last bar is simply a repeat of the second bar.

Example. 9

Now we have taken it in a slightly different direction. Starting off the same but then using the flat-seventh to create a new pattern that's repeated a couple of times.

Example. 10

This has similarities to the original, using some of the same notes minus the triplet timing and with a longer note to end.

Example. 11

Here we have taken the first five notes and then repeated them three times, moving up an octave each time with just a slight rest in-between.

Example. 12

This time we take the previous example but instead of repeating the pattern a third time an octave higher, we give it a simple ending instead.

Altering/changing/playing around with existing patterns/riffs is a good way to create something new. Ultimately we learn by copying from what has been done before, so don't feel that you should be creating new material from thin air by magic, as it really doesn't work like that. When improvising you are drawing upon all the information that you have assimilated and can instantly recall for use. This will be built up of a lot of music that you have learnt from existing material, so using such material to work from is a fine way to develop skills.

Example Patterns To Practice With

Here's a few riffs/patterns to practice creating new things from. I won't include too many here as you can use any boogie-woogie sheet music you have, or alternatively do the same from recorded music if you can learn/play by ear. This is something I would encourage you to learn to do.

Example. 1

Example. 2

Example. 3

Example. 4

Example. 5

Example. 6

Example. 7

Example. 8

Example. 9

Example. 10

See what you can create from these, but then take the idea much further and play around with other music that you have. It's a good way to get started improvising as you have a base to work from.

Listen To Music

Listen To The Music

To take your improvising skills further, by far the best thing to do is to listen to boogie-woogie music. Learn as much as you can from sheet music as well, but it's really important to listen to as much recorded boogie-woogie material as you can, as often as possible. This will internalise the sound you are after, and I can't stress enough how essential it is.

Why Does This Help

When you listen to a lot of music, your brain gets used to how that sounds on a subconscious level. This is useful as once you have learnt the basic rules of what the music is made up off – scales/chords – then you have the tools or information to be able to re-create what you hear on the piano. This should result in a gradual process whereas you improvise, you will naturally re-create some of what you have listened to. I'm not talking about an exact copy necessarily (although that's good) but that internalised sound of the music will find its way to your keyboard as you play and re-create that music.

Patients

Bear in mind that this isn't a quick fix, it's a slow, long-drawn-out process, that won't happen overnight. But if you listen to anyone who has reached a good level of proficiency, then you have someone that has most likely listened and copied. Plus, there's a near unlimited amount of resources (recorded music) to learn from, as opposed to the relatively limited amount of sheet music available. Also, you can learn anything you hear without needing the sheet music for it, which may or may not be available, more likely not in reality. The classic songs are available for sure but anything more modern or obscure you probably won't find available.

Changing Position

If you have a riff that you play in one position on the keyboard, it can sometimes get repetitive if it's played too often. A way around this and to create a little more interest is to repeat the same thing but to move it up (or down) an octave or two. It's still the same pattern of notes, but by changing the position on the keyboard (and so the pitch) it does sound a little different.

Take the little pattern below as an example.

You could repeat this exactly as it is several times in a row, or instead you could switch the position of it each time. One idea isn't better than the other, it's simply another option.

Repeated Once (One Octave Apart)

Repeated Twice (Each One Octave Apart)

Altered Version

You could also repeat the pattern as before, moving up the keyboard an octave at a time and then bring it to a conclusion.

Repeating riff type patterns at different positions is one option, you can also switch octaves while playing more rhythmic chord based parts. It's the same chord (possibly a different inversion if you wish) but moving it an octave or two will make it sound a little different.

Twelve-Bar Example

The next song example employs this idea of jumping around the keyboard. Playing parts in different octave ranges can make the music more interesting, both to listen to and to play. You have a nice long keyboard, so make use of it.

Different Ideas/Options

1.

A 'twiddly' part above, and then moving down for a few chords. You can always move back up again afterward.

2.

Playing chords at different ranges.

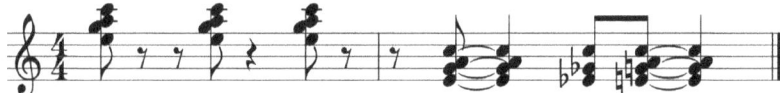

3.

Playing/repeating the same pattern at different ranges.

The example piece also takes a few liberties with the blues twelve-bar chord progression in a couple of places.

- Replacing the '**V**' and '**IV**' chords on bars 9/10 with a '**II**' and '**V**'.

- Replacing '**V**' and '**IV**' chords on bars 9/10 with two '**V**' chords.

- Adding two extra bars at the beginning of a twelve-bar section (two extra '**I**' chords). Although the basic progressions tends to be adhered to, you can take liberties and add additional bars.

Switch The Boogie

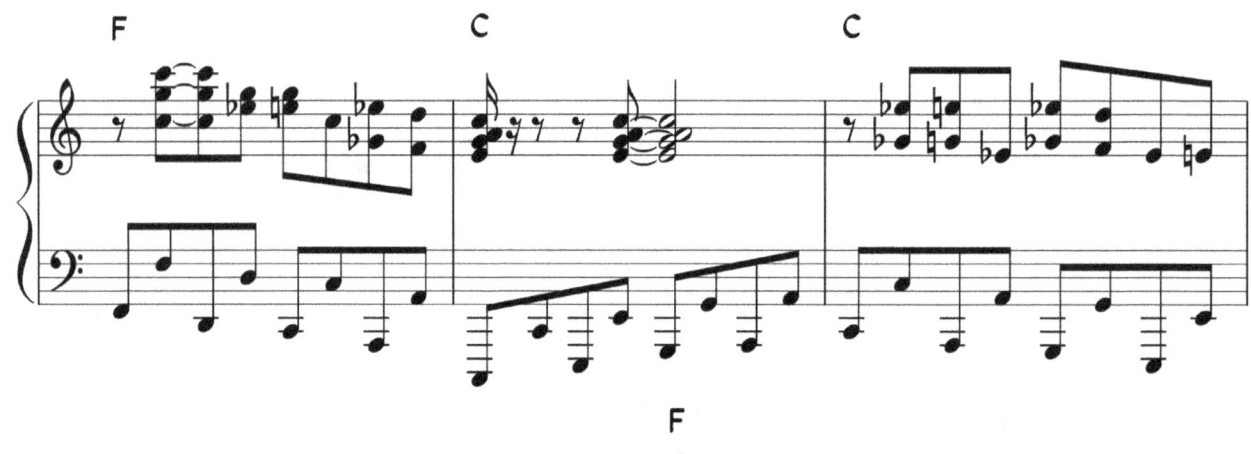

16-Bar Progression

There are other chord progressions that you can use if you wish, so we will take a quick look at some options, starting with the sixteen-bar variety. None of these are as common as the twelve, but they're well worth knowing, and you might have fun playing in a different format.

16-Bar Chord Progression Example

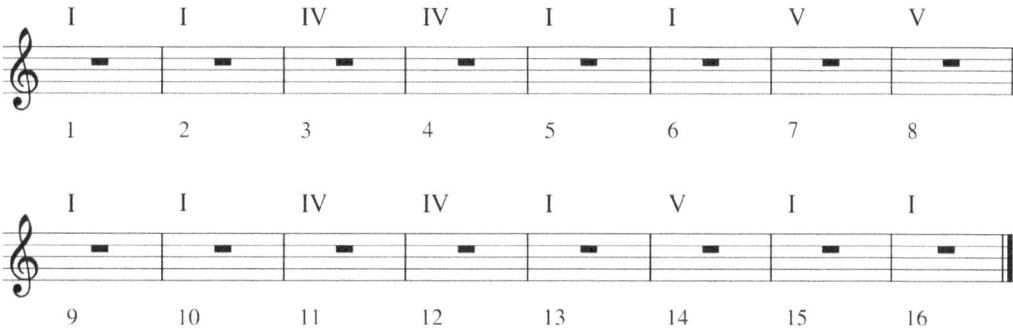

You can see how it jumps to the 'V' chord more often than in a twelve-bar progression. Also notice that unlike the twelve-bar progression it doesn't have the 'V' and 'IV' chords together. It sounds a little different of course and feels different to play, plus it makes a nice change from the usual endless twelve-bars we so typically play.

This can be modified further by adding another (altered) sixteen-bars on to the end of it, creating in essence a thirty-two bar chord progression.

32-Bar Chord Progression Example

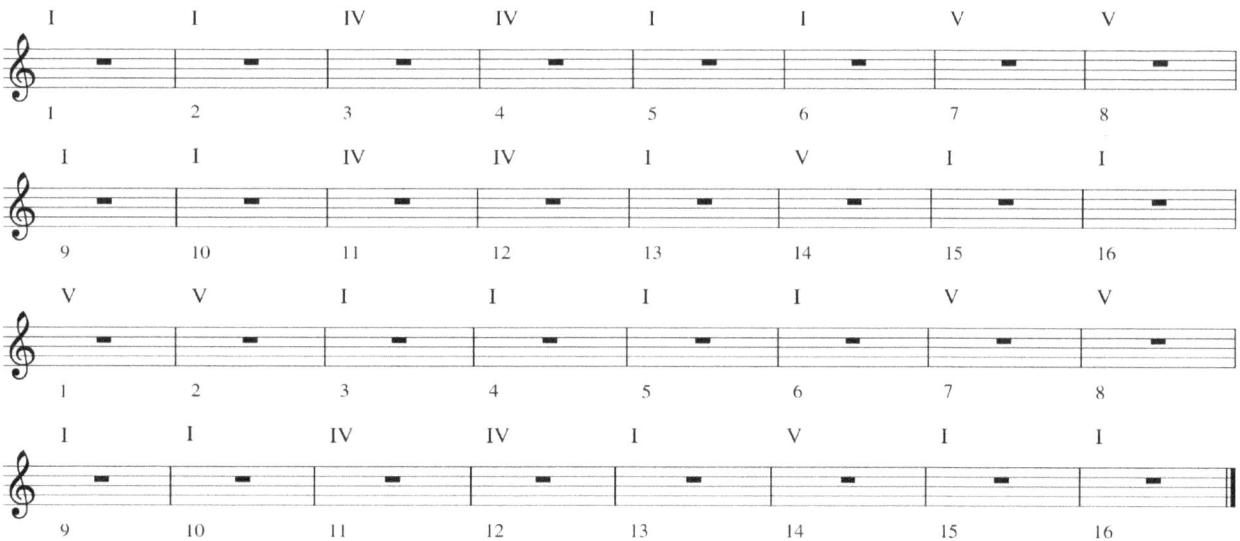

Sixteen Boogie

Thirty-Two Boogie

24-Bar Boogie

Here we have another option that you can play around with. Although the twelve-bar format is the common way of doing things, and we have sixteen bars/thirty-two bars, we also can use a twenty-four bar chord progression.

24-Bar Chord Progression

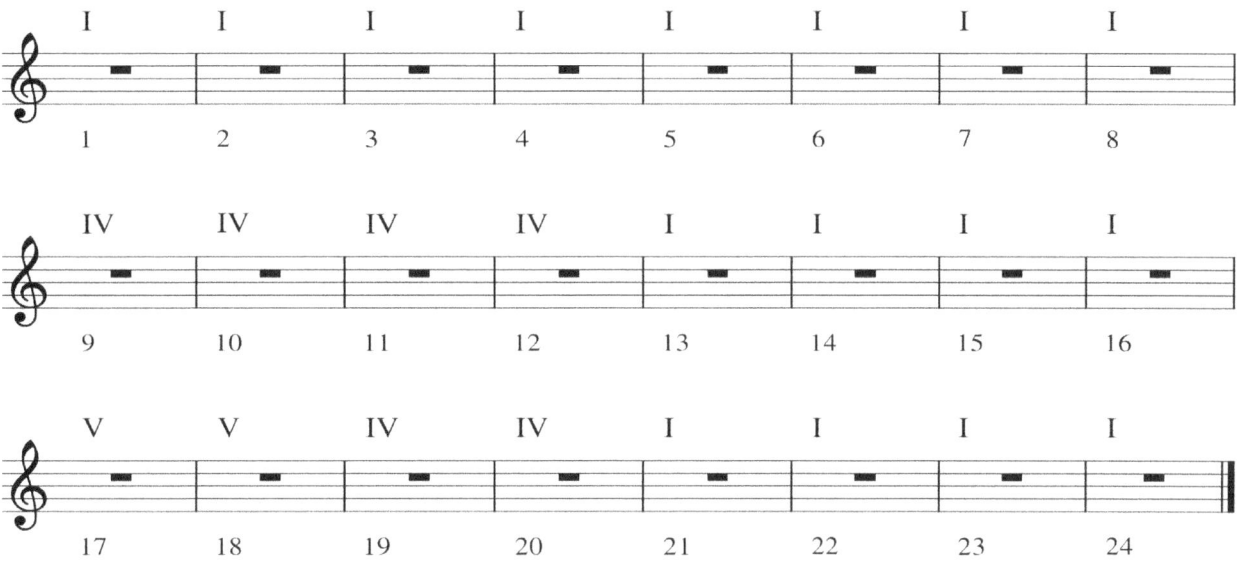

Unlike the sixteen and thirty-two bar chord progression we looked at previously, this isn't so different to the twelve-bar, in-fact it is largely the same. The difference is that it doubles up on all the chords to stretch it out to twice the length. Instead of starting with four bars of the 'I' chord, we have eight. Instead of following with two bars of the 'IV' chord, we have four, and so it continues throughout.

It isn't slower as such, but it does give you more time to play with. More time to develop an idea within each chord or section of the progression. In a sense it's more relaxed, in that you have more time to think, but again, that will depend on what you actually are playing.

Twenty-Four Boogie

Practicing Suggestions

It's pretty obvious that the more time you spend practicing the better you will get, but how much time you spend will be very personal to you, as different peoples spare time will vary a lot. But I will say one thing, consistency is the key.

CONSISTENCY

CONSISTENCY

CONSISTENCY

Yes, in-case I haven't made myself clear, being consistent is quite helpful. It's really helpful in-fact and will make a huge difference to your progression compared to an inconsistent, on and off, practice one week and miss a week kind of affair.

The best way to progress is to practice every day, this would keep the music fresh in your mind. The constant drilling/repetition on a daily basis is how we force the brain to remember and so learn new things. When I say every day, don't panic, it doesn't necessarily mean hours and hours (although if you can, great) but whatever time you can spare. Even ten minutes helps if that's all you have, the main thing is to keep it regular without large gaps in-between. Little and often, is usually far more effective than cramming lots of practice in on just one day and then doing nothing for a week.

Metronome

Using a metronome whilst practicing is highly recommended. The use of one will really help with keeping the timing tight throughout and stop the tempo from drifting too much (although a little is perfectly normal, we aren't machines after-all). When I say metronome, use whatever you have which might be a mechanical metronome, a digital one, even an app on your phone. Playing along to a drum backing is also an option, and sometimes it's even preferable for polishing something you can play, as it adds something to the music and makes it more exciting/interesting and enjoyable.

Listen To The Music

Without doubt one of the most important things you can do when learning a style of music is to listen to it, and I mean a lot, as much as possible. As much as possible without turning yourself mad and ending up hating the music that is.

This may sound obvious, but you really want to make a point of listening to the music that you are trying to play. While you can of course learn songs merely from reading sheet music, the dots and lines really don't convey the feeling of the music the same way, so the brain needs to absorb the sound of the music. This makes it far easier to translate that sound back onto the piano and re-create it. This is in essence how people play by ear and that is another skill that you should want to practice. You can listen to music in two ways.

1.

Listen for the sake of listening, to enjoy it because you obviously like it, but often put on in the background while you are busy. Even though the music might not have one-hundred percent of your attention, by doing this you are still internalizing the sound and feel of that music, probably without even realising it. If you had never even heard a style of music before then you would have a hard timing playing it as you would have no frame of reference, so this really makes a difference.

2.

Listening with your full attention in order to analyze the music with the intention to re-create what you are hearing. Call this playing by ear or transcribing (if you are also copying it down) or whatever you like, but it amounts to the same thing. I would highly recommend you doing this even if it's something you've never tried before, as there is no better way to learn. The best musicians out there learnt by copying what they heard on records rather than just sheet music. Books and sheet music are great tools to help you get started, but something that you learnt by working things out yourself is worth more in real terms, it stays with you and is harder to forget.

Downloadable Audio

Audio files based on the examples within the book are available to download from the website in MP3 format, simply follow the instructions below.

To access and download the MP3 audio files, simply visit the website...

www.tylermusic.co.uk

- Click on audio downloads
- Select relevant book title
- Enter the password shown below
- Click on the download icon

Passwords For Audio

Volume One...   **improvise808boogie**
Volume Two...   **improvise815vol2**
Volume Three...   **vol3improvising822**

Once downloaded, please save them for future use.

Tyler music.co.uk

For further piano books (including spiral bound editions)
sheet music and information on blues
and boogie woogie music
visit the website at…

www.tylermusic.co.uk

**Follow us on Facebook for updates
and information on latest releases.**

Also Available

Improvising Boogie-Woogie Vol. One & Two

Learn to play boogie-woogie like the best of them. If you want to play boogie like Albert Ammons, Axel Zwingenberger or Jools Holland then this is the series for you. The first volume in a series of books to teach boogie-woogie piano, from the basics to more advanced techniques and everything in-between, this will give you the help and material you need.

Improvising Boogie-Woogie Vol. Three

The ultimate guide to playing boogie-woogie continues with volume-three, adding even more left-hand patterns and right-hand riffs to the series. Looking at the use of thirds and sixths, the use of scaler other chord progressions how such riffs are created and how to begin to create your own.

Easy Boogie-Woogie   For Beginners

Easy boogie-woogie takes the beginning boogie pianist through their first steps into the timeless style. It covers the basics with easy to understand clear explanations and includes example pieces throughout that start off easy and gradually increase in difficulty while adding extra elements. With downloadable audio,why not start learning boogie-woogie today.

Easy Boogie-Woogie Vol.2

This second volume of Easy Boogie-Woogie follows on from the first one, taking the beginning boogie player a step further again. New ideas and concepts are introduced along with many examples and explanations throughout. Bigger and better than ever. With downloadable audio to help you along, it's the perfect way to continue your boogie-woogie journey.

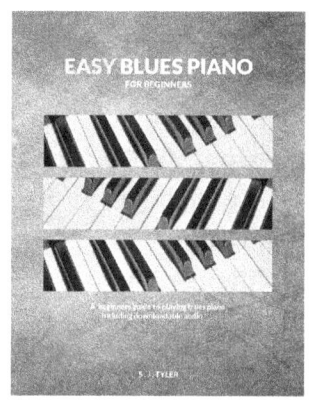

Easy Blues Piano   For Beginners

Learn to play the blues with this beginners guide for the piano. It covers the very basics of the blues, introducing the various elements that create the twelve-bar blues sound. It starts off easy, so even a relative beginner can dive in, and gradually introduces new ideas. With downloadable audio, why not start learning blues today.

Easy New-Orleans   For Beginners

Learn to play that unique style of blues piano from New Orleans, the style of Dr John, Professor Longhair and James Booker to name but a few. Covering everything from chord progressions and left-hand bass patterns and introducing the all important New-Orleans rhythm.

Easy Rock 'N' Roll   For Beginners

Easy rock 'n' roll is for the beginner taking their first steps into the timeless sound of rock 'n' roll piano. Covering the basics with easy to understand clear explanations on how to play in the style of the likes of Jerry Lee Lewis and Little Richard. It includes example pieces throughout that start off easy and gradually increase in difficulty, while adding extra elements along the way. With downloadable audio

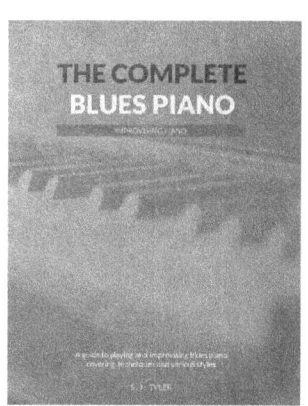

The Complete Blues Piano

The complete blues piano is a comprehensive guide to playing and improvising blues piano. It covers the fundamental principles of the blues and includes in-depth theory and techniques, along with example blues pieces to learn/study with downloadable audio. Ranging from fast boogie-type blues to slow blues, Chicago through to New Orleans, beginners to intermediate, this has it covered.

Piano Blues Scales

The ultimate guide to learning the blues scales for the piano. The scales are clearly shown and explained in all keys for both major and minor scales along with fingering suggestions. But it doesn't stop there, here we go further and include ideas like the combined scales and methods of how to practice and use the scales in a more musical and practical real world fashion.

Bite Sized Specifics – Blues Piano/Walking-Bass

Learn to play the walking-bass for blues piano with the first in a series that concentrates on specific aspects of blues piano. Concentrating on the left-hand, it looks at what the walking-bass is, how it is created and various ways to which you can employ it in a blues environment.

Bite Sized Specifics – Blues Piano/Stride-Piano

Learn to play blues piano using the left-hand stride style. The second in a series that concentrates on a specific aspect of blues piano. Concentrating on the left-hand, it looks at what stride is and how it is created and various ways to which you can employ it in a blues environment.

Bite Sized Specifics – Blues Piano/Right-Hand Vol.1

Learn to play blues piano with the third in a series that concentrates on specific aspects of blues piano. Concentrating on the right-hand, it concentrates on the important aspect of comping, which is the more rhythmic side of blues with an emphasis on the important use of chords and repetitive patterns/riffs that form the backbone of the music.

Tyler Music – Blues & Boogie-Woogie Piano

www.ingramcontent.com/pod-product-compliance
Lightning Source LLC
Chambersburg PA
CBHW081613100526
44590CB00021B/3422